The Field Guide to
# Lighthouses of the
# New England Coast

150 Destinations in Maine, Massachusetts,
Rhode Island, Connecticut, and New Hampshire

Elinor De Wire

Voyageur Press

# Dedication

*To my friend and colleague, lighthouse historian, Jeremy*

First published in 2008 by Voyageur Press, an imprint of MBI Publishing Company, Galtier Plaza, Suite 200, 380 Jackson Street, St. Paul, MN 55101 USA

Voyageur Press titles are also available at discounts in bulk quantity for industrial or sales-promotional use. For details write to Special Sales Manager at MBI Publishing Company, Galtier Plaza, Suite 200, 380 Jackson Street, St. Paul, MN 55101 USA.

To find out more about our books, join us online at www.voyageurpress.com.

ISBN-13: 978-0-7603-2750-0

Editor: Kari Cornell
Designer: Sara Holle

Printed in China

Library of Congress Cataloging-in-Publication Data

De Wire, Elinor, 1953-
The field guide to lighthouses of the New England Coast : 150 destinations in Maine, Massachusetts, Rhode Island, Connecticut, and New Hampshire / Elinor De Wire.
p. cm.
Includes index.
ISBN-13: 978-0-7603-2750-0 (softbound)
ISBN-10: 0-7603-2750-5 (softbound)
1. Lighthouses--New England--Handbooks, manuals, etc. I. Title.
VK1024.N38D39 2007
387.1'550974--dc22

2006022067

**On the Cover:** Rhode Island's Point Judith Light, *Photograph by Susan Cole Kelly*

**On the frontspiece:** Maine's Portland Head Lighthouse, *Photograph by Connie Wiggins*

**On the contents page:** Top left: New Hampshire's Portsmouth Harbor Lighthouse, *Photograph by Shirin Pagels*
Top right: Maine's Bass Harbor Light, *Photograph by Elinor De Wire*
Bottom left: Maine's Rockland Harbor Lighthouse, *Photograph by Elinor De Wire* Bottom right: Connecticut's Stratford Point Lighthouse, *Photograph by Elinor De Wire*

# Contents

# New England: Home to America's First Lighthouse

America's first documented lighthouse went into service in 1716 at Boston, the busiest port in the colonies. The lighthouse survived until the Revolutionary War, when an angry contingent of British sailors lit a keg of gunpowder and tossed it into the tower, leaving behind a pile of rubble. A new tower, still on watch today, was built in 1783. *Photograph by Elinor De Wire*

*There is something about a lighted beacon that suggests hope
and trust and appeals to the better instincts of all mankind.*
Edward Rowe Snow
*The Lighthouses of New England,* 1945

No lighthouses greeted the Pilgrims in 1620 as they arrived in America, landing first on the northern tip of Cape Cod and then at Plymouth. In fact, few lighthouses stood anywhere in the world at this time. But the *Mayflower's* captain was well aware of the need for them. He intended to make landfall much farther south but was diverted to New England because of storms and poor navigational methods. The mishap proved fortunate, since New England had more sheltered harbors and good possibilities for deepwater ports. New England would eventually become a hub of maritime activity and the site for the earliest American lighthouses.

The Narragansetts, Wompanoags, Nausets, and other Native American tribes encountered by the Pilgrims built bonfires on shore to guide their canoes, and New England settlers followed this practice. Little money was sent to the fledgling colonies by their mother country; thus, simple beacons were the only navigational aids that colonists could afford. Colonists built wood fires and hung bails or barrels of flaming pitch. Oil lanterns were placed strategically in windows, on posts, or in church spires. Despite good intentions, these crude lights were sometimes more trouble than help. Mariners often ran aground looking for them.

By 1700, merchants and shipmasters were petitioning England to build lighthouses in the colonies. The Massachusetts Bay Colony seems to have had the most clout, since four lighthouses were built on its shores before the American Revolution. The oldest went into service in 1716 on an island in Boston Harbor. It was funded by a lottery and maintained by a toll paid by passing ships. While it was not the first beacon in North America, historians generally agree it was the first permanent structure to house a light—America's first true lighthouse.

Boston Light was followed by lights at Brandt Point, Beavertail, New London, Plymouth, Portsmouth, and Cape Ann. By 1776, eleven lighthouses stood watch in the colonies, only four of them outside New England. Low construction budgets and a Yankee penchant for thrift meant most were built of cheap materials, such as wood or rubble stone, that soon crumbled and required rebuilding. A few were made to last. The granite lighthouses at New London Harbor, Five Mile Point, Faulkner's Island, Portland Head, and Lynde Point are monuments of strength.

Crude illumination methods were used in the early years of lighthouses, including candles and simple household oil lamps. Keepers were local men, usually men who owned the land on which the lighthouses were built. They often ran the lights as a side job. Some worked for no pay. Overall, the service they provided was sporadic and unreliable, but it was a start.

BEAVER TAIL LIGHT

Beavertail Point, on the tip of Conanicut Island, was one of the early crucial locations for a lighthouse in the American colonies. Ships headed up Narragansett Bay to the busy port at Providence necessitated construction of the first tower in 1749. It stood for more than a century before it was replaced in 1856. *Photograph from the author's collection*

During the American Revolution, New England's lighthouses became pawns of war. Both sides saw them both as a benefit and as a liability. Colonists used light towers to spy on the British but also extinguished lights to prevent aiding the enemy. The British sometimes occupied lighthouses and sometimes destroyed them, too. Boston Light, for example, changed hands several times during the war. In 1775, Americans removed its lamps and set fire to it. A short time later, the British tried to repair the lighthouse but were foiled by troops commanded by Major Benjamin Tupper. The British got revenge a year later when they blew up the tower. It was rebuilt in 1783.

Following American independence, colonial lighthouses were transferred to the new federal government and placed in the hands of the Treasury Department, overseen by Alexander Hamilton. Over the next fifty years, lighthouse administration bounced from agency to agency, and lighthouse construction burgeoned. Though the lighthouse budget was lean, by 1850 about 250 lighthouses stood watch over the nation's shores. More than a third of these were located in New England. The region's dense population, thriving mills and factories, and busy ports made it the center of national activity.

In 1851, responsibility for lighthouses passed into the care of the newly formed U.S. Lighthouse Board. In the wake of severe criticism of American lighthouses, which were considered inferior to those in Europe, this nine-member cadre of military officers, engineers, and scientists set about improving the nation's navigational aids. New England was the center of some of this activity, particularly the research and development of fog signals and marine engineering.

While some parts of the nation, including the Gulf of Mexico and the Pacific Coast, were just beginning to be marked with lighthouses, New England's sentinels were already aging. A massive rebuilding effort began during the 1850s to replace the region's old sentries with new, sturdier, more modern towers. A variety of new technologies were investigated and sometimes implemented. The two sea-swept lighthouses built at Minots Ledge are good examples. In 1851, engineers constructed a modified British design for an iron screwpile tower, only to see it fall during a storm the following year. Undaunted, they applied Scottish technology to a masonry rock lighthouse and successfully built a strong stone tower on the site in 1860.

Equally challenging was caisson technology that allowed the building of offshore lighthouses throughout New England. More than fifty of these lighthouses remain in service. The sturdy stone caisson design of Lake Champlain defied marauding ice floes, while cast-iron telescoping sentinels worked well in saltwater harbors. In fact, iron became the mainstay material of lighthouse construction during the late nineteenth century. Cheap and durable, it was used for lanterns, walls, stairways, platforms, and ancillary buildings like oil houses. The close proximity of foundries in New England made the process easy. Lighthouses were manufactured in pieces, transported to sites, and quickly assembled. They also could be easily moved when necessary.

Along with better towers and foundations came improvements in illumination. Adoption of the Fresnel lens during the 1850s led to the replacement of outdated lighting systems. Whale oil, which had for many years been the primary fuel source, became expensive as the whaling industry declined. Lard oil was dirty and was problematic in cold climates. However, experiments with mineral oil and other fuels were successful. By 1890, almost all New England lighthouses operated Fresnel lenses fueled by kerosene.

The lightkeepers underwent their own occupational evolution under the U.S. Lighthouse Board. Rigorous hiring and training programs were implemented. Keepers wore uniforms and rose through ranks in a quasi-military environment. Regular inspections of the stations were conducted by district offices. Awards for superior service were given by the district superintendents, and severance was doled out to those who failed to meet responsibilities or to adhere to regulations. The result was a regimented and loyal corps of men and women.

The twentieth century brought modernization to New England lighthouses and to the nation's sentinels as a whole. As the Lighthouse Board gave way in 1910 to the Bureau of Lighthouses, the United States touted its coastline as the best marked in the world. Nearly 1,000 sentinels were on watch at this time. New England no longer dominated the maritime community, but it still could claim a fifth of the lighthouses in the nation.

George Putnam, the tough-minded and penurious commissioner of the Bureau of Lighthouses, began tightening the budget and eliminating old technology and unnecessary lights. During the 1920s, he closed up the last of the twin- and triple-light stations, citing them as a careless practice of overlighting for the sake of nostalgia. As shipping needs changed, he abandoned some lights and sold them to private individuals. Others, such as the lights at Monomoy and Marblehead, were replaced by pile design and skeleton towers. Lighthouses were electrified, and modern silent signals, such as radiobeacon, were installed. Automatic devices also came into use under Putnam's reins, portending the eventual obsolescence of the lightkeeper. As if to mollify the thousands of keepers still at work, he secured a much-needed pension plan for lightkeepers.

In 1939, the U.S. Bureau of Lighthouses was dissolved, and navigational aids, including lighthouses, were placed in the care of the U.S. Coast Guard. A new era of modernization and automation began. Many of New England's old lightkeepers segued into the Coast Guard at appropriate ranks; others chose to remain civilians and to finish out their tenure while working alongside Coast Guard keepers. Most stations continued to house families, and operations remained much the same as they had in previous years. A few isolated lighthouses, including Mount Desert Rock, Minots Ledge, Saddleback Ledge, and Duck Island, became "stag stations," where only men served.

Lighthouses that were no longer needed were taken out of service. Some were torn down, whereas others were sold. A few, such as Old Stonington Lighthouse in Connecticut, were passed to historical societies or became centerpieces in public parks. By the 1960s, automation was in full swing. New England lighthouses were made self-sufficient with sensors and timers that operated the lights and with fog signals that were independent of human hands. One by one, keepers were removed and towers and quarters were sealed up against vandalism or were leased or licensed to private groups that would care for them.

Public reaction to these changes was generally negative. Boaters disliked the fact that lightkeepers no longer were available to assist during emergencies or to respond if the lights or fog signals failed. Communities lamented the unattractive physical changes to historic lighthouses wrought by automatic equipment, and the vulnerability of the empty towers to decline and vandalism. Modern aerobeacons were not considered as pretty as Fresnel lenses. Grass wasn't mowed regularly, rust formed on latches and locks, and cobwebs collected around windows.

The last lighthouse keepers were removed from service at Boston Light in 1995. An old and venerable occupation was gone.

Concurrently, a movement to save old lighthouses was gaining momentum. The effort began in earnest in 1966, following the passage of historic preservation legislation that mandated the rescue of all historical properties and associated artifacts. Lighthouses quickly moved near the top of this list. In New England, a Coast Guard officer named Kenneth Black began rescuing lighthouse artifacts—decommissioned lenses, fogbells, tools, logbooks, documents, and more. After retirement, Black opened an exhibit at Rockland's Shore Village Museum (now the Maine Lighthouse Museum). Inspired by his work, others started collecting and exhibiting lighthouse artifacts as well.

The San Francisco–based U.S. Lighthouse Society and the Lighthouse Preservation Society of Massachusetts gave impetus to lighthouse preservation with the conversion of automated and defunct stations to museums, parks, B&Bs, and other uses. The New England Lighthouse Foundation—incorporated during the early 1990s in Wells, Maine, and later expanded to become the American Lighthouse Foundation—took on a similar role. Chapters of these groups formed to address the needs of individual lighthouses.

At the state level, efforts were made to increase public awareness and to ensure that lighthouses were transferred to deserving public entities and made

Experimentation with new light-house designs was the hallmark of the U.S. Lighthouse Board. In 1851, a spider-legged cast-iron tower was built on Minots Ledge, a mile at sea off Cohasset, Massachusetts. This first offshore lighthouse was ill-suited to North Atlantic storms and fell into the sea only a year after its construction. *Photograph from the National Archives*

available to the public. California, Florida, and New Jersey were the leaders in this effort. The 1996 Maine Lights Program unified government officials and the public with the common goal of saving one of the state's most precious assets—its rugged old sentinels.

The Coast Guard was pleased with the enthusiasm and passion exhibited by these nonprofit groups, but budget constraints and the burden of other aspects of its mission meant it could devote little time and few resources to maintaining the sites or preserving their history. With each passing year, resources and manpower to care for lighthouses grew more inadequate. The 9/11 disaster in 2001 was prophetic in terms of tightening the Coast Guard budget and shifting its priorities to homeland security. Fortunately, a solution was found to the lighthouse dilemma before 2001.

The National Historic Lighthouse Preservation Act (NHLPA), enacted in 2000, mandated an appropriate and fair method for transferring ownership of lighthouses to the private sector. It provided a means for loyal and deserving municipal and nonprofit groups to become permanent on-site stewards of the lighthouses they had watched over since automation. The word *lighthouse*, after all, contains the word *house*. A lighthouse was meant to be a home as well as a beacon.

The NHLPA has been a lifeline for old lighthouses. Once, lighthouses saved people in distress. Now, people are saving them. A new kind of lightkeeper has emerged from this heritage-conscious effort. No longer do human hands kindle the wicks of a whale-oil lamp or flip an electrical switch to activate a light; no one stands at the fogbell and hammers an urgent warning signal to a passing ship. Those functions are now automated. But people still do the work necessary to save what is left of a long and colorful chapter in American history. Lenses get polished regularly, windows are washed, stairs are swept, rusty door hinges are replaced, brass is shined, lawns are groomed, and paint is scraped and reapplied. Equally important, visitors are welcomed and a past lifestyle is shared with a generation that has no recollection of lighthouse keeping.

# Let There Be Light!

*At night the island went to its early slumbers, and only the light-house on the hill kept watch. It dazzled the eyes if one looked up, and rendered the darkness more profound.*
E. H. Goss, *Magazine of American History*, September 1884

New England lighthouses are among the oldest sentinels in the nation. Thus, their lanterns have exhibited the full gamut of lighting devices, from feeble candles that required hours to light and maintain, to various types of elaborate lamps and lenses, to the high-tech, reliable, and self-sufficient solar beacons of today.

The earliest lighthouses of the Colonial Era used candelabras as a light source. Boston Light's chandelier of some fifty candles was kindled in 1716. The early lights at Brandt Point and Plymouth also began service with candles. Tapers were difficult to maintain, messy, and a fire hazard. They gave way to lamps by the late 1700s.

Pan lamps, bucket lamps, and spider lamps were the mainstay devices prior to about 1800. They were globeless multi-wick designs. They burned brighter than candles and were easier to maintain. With New England at the hub of the whaling industry, it's no surprise that most lighthouse lamps were cheaply fueled by whale oil. The fuel smelled foul and exuded sticky soot the lightkeepers had to clean off the lantern windows. Lard oil also was popular, but it was dirty and congealed in cold weather.

The classical lenses he invented still shine from many lighthouse lanterns, including Boston Light. *Photograph by Elinor De Wire*

French physicist Jean-Augustin Fresnel devised a superior lighthouse lens in 1823 that supplanted earlier reflector systems and increased light range as much as threefold at some sites. *Photograph from the U.S. Lighthouse Society*

By the nineteenth century, the French had developed the Argand Lamp, named for its designer, physicist Francois-Pierre Ami Argand. Glass globes, called chimneys, and a hollow wick that funneled air to the flame helped the Argand Lamp burner steadier, brighter, and cleaner. Also part of the scheme was a silvered, parabolic (bowl-shaped) reflector placed behind each lamp to intensify its light.

This design was modified in 1812 by Winslow Lewis of Cape Cod. A shipmaster in his youth, Lewis often had bemoaned the poor lights exhibited along America's coast. When an embargo during the War of 1812 forced him out of the shipping business, he sought other means to support his family. A large measure of confidence and a little Yankee ingenuity told him he could design a better lighthouse beacon.

In an act that today might be labeled patent infringement, Lewis copied Argand's design and added a small lens in front of each lamp. Later, he copied the work of other inventors of the day and incorporated it into his designs. He patented his apparatus as the "Magnifying and Reflecting Lantern," but the onerous name soon became known to the maritime world as the Lewis light. It was not a good design, since Lewis had little knowledge of the physics of light, and the lenses and reflectors he manufactured were poor quality. Nonetheless, his intentions were noble. He managed to convince the U.S. Lighthouse Establishment to contract with him for the outfitting of nearly every lighthouse built between 1815 and 1845.

While Lewis was cornering the American market for lighthouse illumination, another French scientist was perfecting a lenticular device called the Fresnel lens. Physicist Jean-Augustin Fresnel was charged with improving the rugged, sea-swept lighthouses of the French coast. He succeeded in 1823 with a series of prismatic lenses that focused and magnified a single light source. He continued to use an oil lamp but surrounded it with a beehive-shaped lens composed of refracting prisms, magnifying panels or bull's-eyes, and mirrors.

Once refined, the Fresnel lens became available in six orders, or sizes, and two primary types—fixed and flashing. Fixed lenses did not revolve and had a central barrel of smooth magnifying glass through which the light was focused and projected out to sea. Flashing lenses revolved around the light source on chariot wheels, bearings, or in mercury floats (tubs of high-density, low-friction mercury). Bull's-eyes of concentric rings of magnifying glass created the flashes as the lens turned.

First-order lenses were the largest and most powerful and were used for seacoast lights. Sixth-orders were the least powerful and also the smallest. They were installed in channel and river lights. In between, second- through fifth-orders marked harbors and ports with varying degrees of brilliance. Years after Fresnel's work, a 3.5-order lens was developed. In the 1880s, Chance Brothers of England built a gigantic hyper-radiant lens, the largest ever produced. Only one of these was purchased by the United States for service in Hawai'i.

In New England prior to 1880, whale oil and lard oil were the primary lamp fuels. As the coal industry grew, mineral oil, or kerosene, gained widespread usage. It was compressed into a gas about 1890 and used in incandescent oil vapor lamps. Acetylene gas also was used in some lamps. It could be stored in tanks, and a special actuator valve was designed that responded to sunlight. The device portended automation, but it was electricity that gave the final impetus toward self-sufficiency.

Electric lights gained widespread usage after 1900 and were installed in most New England lights by 1940. Fresnel lenses adapted well to this new, clean light source. Mainland stations were connected to electric power lines, while submarine cables brought power to islands and rock lighthouses. Backup generators ensured there would be power if the lines failed. America was

Others are displayed in museums. The lens from Matinicus Light is on exhibit in the Maine Lighthouse Museum. *Photograph by Sue Lott*

ready for a keeperless lighthouse, but it took years for the maritime world to warm to the idea.

In the 1960s, the Coast Guard moved forward with alacrity. Reliable equipment had been developed, and a strapped budget demanded cuts. Lighthouse keepers had to go. Automation brought modern acrylic and plastic lenses to lighthouses. These compact, durable designs employed the same principles of refraction and magnification as the classical Fresnel lenses, but without the massive size, expense, and labor. Light sensors activated the lights at dark or in fog and extinguished them at dawn. Sealed, contained units kept out bugs and dirt and required no lantern for protection or keeper to tend them each day. Ultimately, even the power source was confined cheaply and renewably with solar collectors and batteries.

*Technology now switches on the light,*
*And times the beam that penetrates the night.*
*We've gained a long-sought economic goal;*
*Retained the Harbor light but lost its soul.*
Lawrence Anderson, *The Harbor Light*

## Chapter 1

# The Lighthouses
# of Maine

Often cited as Maine's "most photographed lighthouse," the quaint Cape Neddick Light combines all the elements of a pretty light station—conical tower, Victorian keeper's quarters, oil house, and white picket fence. *Photograph by Elinor De Wire*

# Baker Island Lighthouse
## ISLESFORD

The first sentinel to mark the tricky passage through Cranberry Islands on the approach to Somes Sound was a wooden tower erected in 1828 on Baker Island. President John Quincy Adams authorized the lighthouse, which operated with whale-oil lamps and reflectors. By 1855, however, the lighthouse and keeper's home were badly deteriorated.

**FOR MORE INFORMATION**
Acadia National Park
P.O. Box 177
Bar Harbor, ME 04609
207.288.3338
acad1@us-national-parks.net

A new lighthouse was commissioned that year by the Lighthouse Board. The tower was 43 feet tall and exhibited a fourth-order Fresnel illuminated with lard-oil lamps. The light shone from 105 feet above sea level. It was connected to a Cape Cod–style keeper's dwelling by a covered passageway.

In 1903, the tower began to weaken and was stabilized with an exterior sheath of new brick. The light was manned until 1966, when a modern optic replaced the Fresnel lens. The Fresnel lens is now displayed in the Fishermen's Museum at Pemaquid Point.

The lighthouse is accessible from Acadia National Park only by boat. The tour schedule varies and is offered only in summer. Bar Harbor Whale Watch Company now runs the tours: www.barharborwhales.com.

One of the highlights of a naturalist-led cruise and hike in Acadia National Park is the 1855 Baker Island Lighthouse. Adventuresome visitors can walk to the lighthouse at low tide from Little Cranberry Island. *Photograph by Jeremy D'Entremont*

# Bass Harbor Head Lighthouse
## MOUNT DESERT ISLAND

**FOR MORE INFORMATION**
See Baker Island Lighthouse

**DIRECTIONS**
From the town of Northeast Harbor, take ME 198 north and then ME 102 and ME 102A south through Bass Harbor to the parking area next to the lighthouse.

A treacherous bar extending across one side of the entrance to Blue Hill Bay and Bass Harbor necessitated construction of a lighthouse in 1858. The picturesque brick sentinel stood 32 feet tall and perched on a ledge overlooking Bass Harbor. A keeper's dwelling was attached to the tower, and a fogbell stood in front of the tower.

The bell was moved to a brick bell house in 1876. Two years later, some work was done to the keeper's house. A boathouse was built in 1894, and a barn and an oil house were added in 1905. They remain standing.

Today the lighthouse still operates, exhibiting a red occulting beacon from a fourth-order Fresnel lens that was installed in 1902. The original bell was replaced by a larger 4,000-pound bell in 1898. The station was automated in 1974.

The grounds of the station are open year-round from 9:00 AM until sunset. The house is a private home occupied by a Coast Guard family.

Blue water, jagged rocks, and emerald evergreens add to the rugged ambience of the 1858 Bass Harbor Lighthouse. Its occulting red beacon is a marker for Blue Hill Bay. *Photograph courtesy of National Oceanic & Atmospheric Administration*

# Bear Island Lighthouse
## NORTHEAST HARBOR

The original lighthouse, built in 1839 to mark the entrance to Northeast Harbor, was a wooden tower incorporated into a stone keeper's dwelling. It was rebuilt in 1853 as a 31-foot-tall brick tower attached to one end of the old dwelling. The lighthouse lasted until 1889, when it was completely rebuilt.

The new station consisted of a 33-foot-tall brick tower and attached workroom, a separate dwelling for the keeper, a barn, and a boathouse. The lantern exhibited a fifth-order Fresnel lens. A brick oil house was added in 1905.

In 1982, the Coast Guard discontinued the light after offshore lighted buoys took over its duties. In 1987, the station became the property of Acadia National Park. With the help of the Friends of Acadia, the property was restored and the tower was relit in 1989. The National Park Service then leased the station to a private owner. The lighthouse is not open to the public but can be seen from a boat cruise offered from Northeast Harbor during the summer.

**FOR MORE INFORMATION**
See Baker Island Lighthouse.

An image from the 1886 book *All Among the Lighthouses* featured a pleasant summer day at Bear Island Lighthouse. Winter was much less agreeable, with the family often cut off from civilization, forced to ration provisions, and miserably cold. *Photograph from the author's collection*

# Blue Hill Bay Lighthouse
## BROOKLIN

L ocated on Green Island, which is barely visible during high tide, the Federal-style lighthouse was completed in 1857 to assist vessels plying the busy lumber port of Ellsworth. It is sometimes called Eggemoggin Light, since it also guides vessels into Eggemoggin Reach.

The brick tower was cylindrical and whitewashed to help it show against the backdrop of sea. It exhibited a fourth-order Fresnel lens fueled by whale-oil lamps. The tower was attached to a keeper's dwelling by a brick passageway. There was also a fogbell on the station.

In 1905, a barn, a boathouse, and a privy were built. That same year, the lamps were converted to kerosene, and a brick oil house was added to store the incendiary fuel. Thirty years later, the lighthouse was decommissioned and its beacon was transferred to a steel skeleton tower.

The lighthouse was sold to a private party years ago and remains in private hands. It is not open to the public.

Extensive tidepools surround the 1857 Blue Hill Bay Lighthouse. It is one of Maine's more remote sentinels, decommissioned in 1933 and now privately owned. *Photograph by Jeremy D'Entremont*

# Boon Island Lighthouse
## YORK

Boon Island received it name after castaways from a 1682 shipwreck took refuge there. They were rescued after setting a fire that was seen from shore, nine miles away. The island was considered a boon to their survival.

Small and inhospitable, Boon Island received its unlighted aid to navigation in 1799. The 50-foot wooden tower, called a day-beacon, lasted only four years before a storm toppled it. A stone daymark was hastily built to replace the original, but it fell in an 1811 storm. Another tower, this one lighted, was demolished by the sea in 1831.

A fourth beacon was constructed in 1832 but was in a dilapidated condition by 1852. The newly empowered U.S. Lighthouse Board decided a strong tower was needed and appropriated $25,000 for the project. A sturdy granite tower on a heavy foundation was completed in 1855. The new tower stood 133 feet tall and had a second-order Fresnel lens illuminated by whale-oil lamps. Within thirty years, the area's notorious wind and waves had begun to shake the lighthouse during storms, so in 1885, six long tie rods were bolted to the exterior from top to bottom.

Storms continued to pummel the station. In 1978, after a severe winter storm damaged the keeper's dwelling and forced the keeper to take refuge in the tower, the Coast Guard opted to repair the station and to automate it. The keeper's dwelling was later burned down by the Coast Guard. The lighthouse lens was removed in 1993 and is now on display in the Kittery Historical and Naval Museum.

The lighthouse was licensed to the American Lighthouse Foundation in 2000. It is only accessible by boat.

**FOR MORE INFORMATION**
American Lighthouse Foundation
P.O. Box 889
Wells, ME 04090
207.646.0245
www.lighthousefoundation.org

Boon Island Light, nine miles off the coast of southern Maine, was a lonely and dangerous assignment prior to modern methods of communication and travel, a fact not apparent in this 1910 image from a collectors' card. *Photograph from the author's collection*

# Brown's Head Lighthouse
## VINALHAVEN

**DIRECTIONS**
Take the ferry from Rockland to Vinalhaven. After exiting the ferry, turn right onto Main Street. Turn left on High Street and then right on North Haven Road. Turn left on Crockett River Road (a dirt road), then right on the second dirt road, and drive past a cemetery to the lighthouse parking area.

Built in 1832 to serve ships loaded with granite from local quarries, the diminutive 20-foot-tall stone tower held a fifth-order Fresnel light fueled by whale-oil lamps. It marked the western entrance to Fox Islands Thorofare. In 1857, the lighthouse was repaired and a new keeper's dwelling was built. The U.S. Lighthouse Establishment also added a 1,000-pound fogbell at this time.

In 1902, the station was upgraded with a fourth-order Fresnel lens, and in 1987, it was automated. The lens remains operative, but the fogbell was deactivated and given to Vinalhaven Historical Museum. An electric horn replaced the fogbell. In 1996, the lighthouse and grounds were transferred to the town of Vinalhaven. It is maintained as a private residence and is not open to the public, but the grounds are open to visitors.

Heavy summer fogs in Penobscot Bay that hindered ships carrying local granite convinced President Andrew Jackson to authorize construction of Brown's Head Lighthouse in 1832. It was rebuilt in 1857 and was photographed circa 1885 with its lightkeeping families. *Photograph from the Coast Guard Archives*

# Burnt Coat Harbor Lighthouse
## Swan's Island

The station, which takes its name from explorer Samuel de Champlain—who called it Brule-Cote, or "Burnt Coast"—began in 1872 as two range lights on Hockomock Head to mark the entrance to Burnt Coat Harbor. In 1884, the front light was discontinued and was eventually razed.

The remaining square brick tower continued to serve with a fifth-order Fresnel lens. It was connected to the keeper's dwelling by a covered walkway. An oil house was added in 1895 when the fuel was changed from lard oil to kerosene. A fogbell went into service in 1911 and was later replaced by a foghorn.

In 1975, the light was discontinued and

**FOR MORE INFORMATION**
Town of Swan's Island
P.O. Box 11
Swan's Island, ME 04685

**DIRECTIONS**
The island is poorly marked with signs, so it is best to stop at a local business along the ferry road to get directions to the lighthouse.

moved to a nearby skeleton tower. Complaints about the unsightly skeleton tower resulted in the return of the beacon to the lighthouse a few years later. In 1982, the tower's paint was removed and a clear sealant was sprayed on the brown tower. More complaints ensued, whereupon the tower was painted white.

The light station became the property of the town of Swan's Island in 1994, and the buildings are gradually being restored. The lighthouse is not open for touring, but the grounds are part of a public park. The island is accessible by a ferry that runs from Bass Harbor to Swan's Island.

Overlooking what some nineteenth-century ship-masters considered the best small harbor in eastern Maine, Burnt Coat Harbor Light has stood watch since 1872. It greets visitors arriving on the ferry from Bass Harbor to Swan's Island. *Photograph from Jeremy D'Entremont's collection*

# Burnt Island Lighthouse
## BOOTHBAY HARBOR

**FOR MORE INFORMATION**
Maine Department
of Marine Resources
P.O. Box 8
West Boothbay Harbor, ME 04575
207.633.2284
www.maine.gov/dmr/education/
lighthousetour.htm

**HOURS OF OPERATION**
A three-hour program is offered
during the summer from Monday
through Friday, twice daily at 10 AM
and 12:45 PM The Novelty, located at
Pier 8 in Boothbay Harbor, serves as
the ferry to the island.

**DIRECTIONS**
From US 1, two miles east of
Wiscasset, take ME 27 to
Boothbay Harbor and turn right on
Union Street. Go right again on
Atlantic Avenue, which turns into
Grand View Road. The lighthouse
is visible from several spots along
this road, but better views are
offered by sightseeing cruises in
Boothbay Harbor.

Marking the west side of the entrance to Boothbay Harbor, this lighthouse was inaugurated in 1821 with whale-oil lamps and reflectors. Constructed of fieldstone and brick, the 30-foot tower was attached to a wooden dwelling. In 1857, the dwelling was torn down and rebuilt with a covered walkway connected to the lighthouse. The tower's lantern was enlarged to hold a fourth-order Fresnel lens.

In 1880, a boathouse was built. A dark sector was added to the light's characteristic flashing pattern in 1888 to prevent confusion with nearby Cuckolds Light. Complaints by mariners entering Boothbay Harbor led to a complete change from a fixed white beam to a fixed red beam with two white sectors. After kerosene became the lamp's fuel during the 1890s, a slate oil house was constructed to store it. A fogbell and pyramidal bell house were added in 1895.

In 1962, the lighthouse was electrified— the last lighthouse in New England to be modernized. It was automated in 1989 with a modern optic. Its old lens is now displayed at the Maine Lighthouse Museum in Rockland.

Burnt Island Lighthouse Society maintained the lighthouse property from 1980 until 1988. Today it is owned and managed by the Maine Department of Marine Resources. It is accessible only by boat.

The fishing fleet at Boothbay Harbor benefited from the establishment of Burnt Island Lighthouse. It was a popular family station during its manned years, due to the proximity of the village of Boothbay and the quiet beauty of the island. Today, it serves as both a navigational aid and as an educational site for the Maine Department of Marine Resources. *Photograph from the author's collection*

# Cape Elizabeth Lighthouse
## CAPE ELIZABETH

A daymark was placed on Cape Elizabeth in 1811 after a shipwreck claimed many lives. It was razed in 1828 to make way for twin light towers.

Believing that one light was sufficient, the U.S. Lighthouse Board discontinued the west tower in 1855. Mariners complained bitterly, and the light was restored. In 1865, the west tower was painted with a vertical red stripe, and the east tower with four horizontal red bands. There was also a fog whistle in service by this time.

By 1874, the rubble stone towers were deteriorating. They were replaced by two comely 67-foot-tall cast-iron lighthouses of Italianate design, standing 300 yards apart. Each lighthouse exhibited a second-order Fresnel lens. One light showed a fixed beacon, and the other light flashed. A roaring fog siren replaced the whistle.

**FOR MORE INFORMATION**
American Lighthouse
Foundation
P.O. Box 889
Wells, ME 04090
207.646.0245
www.lighthousefoundation.org

**DIRECTIONS**
From US 1 in Scarborough, take ME 207 southeast to ME 77. Drive five miles to Two Lights State Park, turn right onto Two Lights Road, and follow Two Lights Road to its end.

In 1924, the west tower was decommissioned. The east tower was automated in the 1960s and continues in service with a modern beacon. Its second-order lens is on display in the Cape Elizabeth Town Hall.

In 2000, the lighthouse was leased to the American Lighthouse Foundation, which has begun restoration efforts. It is not open to the public but can be viewed from a nearby parking area at the end of Two Lights Road.

Made nationally famous during the 1920s by artist Edward Hopper's painting *Two Lights*, the twin sentinels at Cape Elizabeth were well-known locally because of light-keeper Marcus Hanna's brave rescue of the crew of the wrecked schooner *Australia* in 1885. Hanna was awarded a lifesaving medal and has been honored with a Coast Guard buoy tender that bears his name. Only one tower at Cape Elizabeth remains active today. *Photograph by Yvonne Zemotel*

# Cape Neddick Lighthouse
## YORK

**FOR MORE INFORMATION**
Friends of Nubble Light
P.O. Box 9
York, ME 03909
207.363.1040

**DIRECTIONS**
From US 1A at York, turn onto
Nubble Road and follow signs
for Nubble Light.

This picturesque lighthouse stands a short distance off York on an islet called the Nubble. It is one of the nation's most photographed sentinels. It began service in 1879 to mark the entrance to the York River. The 41-foot-tall cast-iron lighthouse was connected to a keeper's dwelling by a covered walkway. It displayed a red fourth-order beacon. A 1,200-pound fogbell suspended on a pyramidal wooden tower provided the sound signal.

In 1891, after the fourth-order Fresnel lens was damaged, the lens was replaced by a new one. The switch to kerosene fuel necessitated the addition of an oil house, which was completed in 1902 and was painted red. The station was electrified in 1938 and automated in 1987. An electric horn replaced the old fogbell.

In 1977, a digitized image of the lighthouse was chosen for inclusion in a time capsule aboard the *Voyager II* space probe. Along with other Earth artifacts, it is intended to convey the nature of our world to other civilizations that may exist in the universe.

The lighthouse is owned by the town of York. It is decorated in holiday lights every December and for a summertime festival called "Christmas in July." Though not accessible to the public, it is easily viewed from Soheir Park.

Cape Neddick, nicknamed the Nubble Light for its tiny jutting islet, is one of Maine's major tourist attractions. Its image appears on a variety of souvenirs and was included in a canister aboard the *Voyager II* space probe. The quaint station is decorated with lights every December. (**Left**: *Photograph by Yvonne Zemotel*; **Right**: *Photograph by Jonathan De Wire*)

# Cuckolds Lighthouse
## SOUTHPORT

Circa 1874, a wooden tripod daymark was placed on a rock ledge known as Cuckolds. It marked Cape Newagen and the entrance to the Sheepscot River. The site was named for a place along England's Thames River that was once owned by a gentleman with an unfaithful wife. A century after the daymark was set up, a fog signal house made of stone was built in the same spot to provide steam for a fog trumpet.

In 1907, the building was increased to 48 feet in height, a lantern was added, and a fourth-order Fresnel lens was installed—thus the Cuckolds became a lighthouse. An attached keeper's house was constructed nearby. The station had its woes, however. Its low elevation made it vulnerable to storm waves, and it was nearly destroyed in a 1933 storm. The Coast Guard razed the keeper's dwelling in 1977.

By the time the dwelling was razed, the light had been automated with a modern optic and its lens had been transferred to the Shore Village Museum (now the Maine Lighthouse Museum) in Rockland. The lighthouse is not open to the public, but it can be viewed from the shore. It is owned and managed by an organization called the Cuckolds Fog Signal and Light Station Council.

**DIRECTIONS**
At the junction of ME 27 and ME 228 at the south end of Cape Newagen, turn southeast onto an unnamed road with a sign for Town Landing. Continue about a quarter mile to the public pier. The lighthouse is visible just offshore. It can also be seen from some of the sightseeing cruises that depart from Boothbay Harbor and Bath.

Perched on a rocky ledge thought to have been named for a jilted Englishman, Cuckolds Light is perhaps New England's oddest-shaped sentinel. A spacious dwelling adjoined the round tower and fog signal house until 1977, when the Coast Guard demolished it.
*Photograph by Sue Lott*

# Curtis Island Lighthouse
## CAMDEN

The station was originally established as a brick tower in 1836. It was called Negro Island Light, after a black cook who lived on the five-acre islet. The keeper's dwelling was rebuilt in 1889, at which time a barn and boathouse were also added. An oil house was built in 1895.

The lighthouse was torn down and reconstructed a year later. The 25-foot-tall cylindrical brick tower with attached workroom was in the Federal style. It exhibited a fourth-order Fresnel lens. In 1934, the name of the island was changed to Curtis Island, in honor of well-known Camden resident Cyrus H. K. Curtis, publisher of the *Saturday Evening Post.*

The station was automated in 1972 and leased to the town of Camden. Its fogbell was removed, and the lens was moved to the Camden Public Library. The lighthouse site on Curtis Island is a town park, but there is no public access to the island. You can see the lighthouse from a private boat or from a number of scenic cruises leaving Camden Harbor in the summer.

The 1896 Curtis Island Light—the second tower to serve at the site—adds an aura of romance and mystery to the nearby town of Camden. Several movies have been filmed in the area, and the comely tower with its bright green beacon is a favorite with boaters and photographers. *Photograph by Sue Lott*

# Deer Island Thorofare Lighthouse
## STONINGTON

Also called Mark Island Light, this station began service in 1857. The 25-foot-tall square brick tower was fitted with a fourth-order Fresnel lens. The station also included a wooden keeper's dwelling and a fogbell. A boathouse and an oil house were added a few years later.

The station was automated in 1958, and the lens was replaced by a small plastic beacon. All structures except the lighthouse were razed. In 1998, the tower was transferred to the Island Heritage Trust. Mark Island then became a wildlife refuge.

The lighthouse is not open to the public.

Mark Island Light, near Stonington, Me.

Deer Island Thorofare Light, also called Mark Island Light, was a pleasant family station, but winter weather often created problems. In February 1935, lightkeeper Elmer Conary suffered a heart attack during a particularly cold period when ice surrounded the station. Flares were sent up to alert the mainland of the emergency. A tug rammed through the ice to bring a doctor to the lighthouse, then took Conary back to the mainland for treatment. *Photograph from Jeremy D'Entremont's collection*

# Dice Head Lighthouse
## CASTINE

**FOR MORE INFORMATION**
Town of Castine
P.O. Box 204
Castine, ME 04221
207.326.4502

**DIRECTIONS**
From US 1 in Orland, turn right onto ME 175. Turn south on ME 166 and continue to Castine. Turn right on Battle Avenue and drive about two miles to the lighthouse.

First lighted in 1838 with a Lewis light, the sentinel marked the entrance to the Penobscot River. It was constructed of rough rubble stone. A handsome wooden keeper's house stood nearby.

In 1858, the tower was encased in wood, and a passageway was added to connect it to the keeper's quarters. The beacon was changed to a fourth-order lens fueled by whale oil. The wood sheath around the tower was removed during the 1870s. A barn was added to the station in 1888.

By the early twentieth century, shipping had decreased on the Penobscot River. The lighthouse was extinguished in 1937. The buildings were deeded to the town of Castine, which rented out the keeper's dwelling until 1990, using the income to maintain the site. In 1999, the keeper's dwelling caught fire. Repairs were made, and the house continues to be rented. The grounds are open year-round.

During a blizzard in 1929, the Dice Head Lighthouse gave guidance to a lost airplane pilot. He showed his gratitude a few weeks later by flying over the station and dropping Christmas gifts for the lightkeeper. The gesture gave rise to the "Flying Santa of the Lighthouses," an organized program of holiday gift-giving to families at lonely light stations.
*Photograph by Yvonne Zemotel*

# Eagle Island Lighthouse
## DEER ISLAND

The 260-acre island, located in East Penobscot Bay, received a lighthouse in 1839 to guide the region's many lumber ships. The stone tower exhibited a Lewis light fueled by whale oil. A wooden residence stood adjacent to the lighthouse, and a fogbell operated by clockwork also was built.

In 1858, the 30-foot tower was updated with a new cast-iron stairway and a fourth-order Fresnel lens. The optic remained unchanged until the 1890s, when it was converted to kerosene. An oil house was built in 1895 to house the incendiary fuel.

Although pristine and scenic, the station was isolated, and the winter cold was hard on the keepers. Most kept livestock and gardened in order to augment their provisions. No boat was provided until 1917. There was no plumbing or electricity until the late 1940s.

The station was automated in 1959 with a modern optic and fog signal, and all buildings except the tower were put up for auction. There were no bidders, so in 1964 the Coast Guard burned down all the buildings except the lighthouse and the fogbell tower. When the Coast Guard tried to move the 4,200-pound fogbell ashore, it accidentally rolled into the sea. It was later retrieved and put on display on Great Spruce Head Island.

What remained of the station was transferred to the nonprofit Eagle Island Light Caretakers in 1998. The group maintains the property but has not opened it to the public. It is not visible from shore.

Many lighthouse families suffered hardships on island stations. The 1839 Eagle Island Light had no boat provided until 1929, no well for water until 1947, and no indoor plumbing until 1949. *Photograph from the Historic American Buildings Survey*

# Egg Rock Lighthouse
## WINTER HARBOR

**DIRECTIONS**
From Ellsworth, follow ME 3 east to the entrance of Acadia National Park. Drive east from the park visitor center to Park Loop Road. On this 20-mile loop, stop at any of the following sites to view the offshore lighthouse: Champlain Mountain Overlook, the Precipice, or the Scenic Overlook. It can also be seen from a number of sightseeing cruises and whale-watching tours departing from Bar Harbor. There are special lighthouse cruises that offer a close view.

Guarding the northern waters of Frenchman Bay, the 40-foot brick lighthouse was incorporated into the roof of a wood dwelling. It was constructed in 1875 at a cost of $15,000. The optic was a fifth-order Fresnel lens. The station also included a fogbell mounted in a pyramidal tower and fitted with an automatic striker. The bell tower, destroyed in a winter storm during 1887, was replaced by a wooden frame tower.

A fourth-order Fresnel lens was installed in 1902 to increase the light's range. The lighthouse was automated in 1976. The lantern was removed and an exposed aerobeacon took the place of the old classical lens. Public outcry over the loss of the lantern caused the Coast Guard to construct a new lantern in 1986.

In 1998, the light station was transferred to the U.S. Fish and Wildlife Service. It is now part of the Maine Coastal Islands National Wildlife Refuge. The buildings are not open to the public. The lighthouse can be seen in the distance from several points within Acadia National Park.

The integral design of Egg Rock Light combined the house with the tower. During the 1890s, the house was expanded with a raised roof and dormers on a small second story. The pyramidal structure to the right of the lighthouse was a bell tower for the fogbell. *Photograph from the author's collection*

# Fort Point Lighthouse
## STOCKTON SPRINGS

Fort Pownall, established in 1759 to guard against French invasion, gave its name to Fort Point. The first lighthouse on the point was a stone tower built in 1836 to guide vessels into the Penobscot River and the lumber and potato ports at Stockton Springs and Bangor. It was flanked by a small dwelling. The lighthouse was illuminated with oil lamps and reflectors.

The station was rebuilt in 1857. A 31-foot square brick tower was attached to a two-story wooden keeper's dwelling. In the 1890s, a pyramidal tower was added to hold a fogbell, and the light was converted to kerosene. A brick oil house was built to store the fuel. The lighthouse and fog signal were automated in 1988, but the Fresnel lens was left in place. Other than a few modifications to modernize it, the station remains much as it was during the early twentieth century.

The station is part of Fort Point State Park and Historic Site. The grounds are open during park hours from sunrise to sunset.

**FOR MORE INFORMATION**
Fort Point State Historic Site
c/o Bureau of Parks and Lands
106 Hogan Road
Bangor, ME 04401
207.567.3356

**DIRECTIONS**
From US 1 in Stockton Springs, follow signs for Fort Point State Park.

Old and new technologies merge in the square brick tower and lantern of Fort Point Light. Although its 1857 prism lens remains in use, a modern acrylic beacon on a pole waits on standby as a backup. *Photograph by Yvonne Zemotel*

# Franklin Island Lighthouse
## FRIENDSHIP

**FOR MORE INFORMATION**
Maine Coastal Islands National
Wildlife Refuge
P.O. Box 279
Milbridge, Maine 04658
207.546.2124

Ordered built by President Thomas Jefferson in 1803, the lighthouse was not completed until 1807 due to difficulty obtaining materials. Its purpose was to mark rocks in the vicinity of the entrance to the St. George River. The lantern was illuminated with spider lamps until about 1820, at which time it was refitted with a Lewis light.

By 1831, the station needed to be rebuilt. Apparently work on the second tower was insufficient, and a third tower was built in 1855. The sturdy 45-foot-tall brick lighthouse held a fourth-order Fresnel lens. The tower was connected to a wooden keeper's dwelling. In 1895, after the beacon was converted to kerosene, an oil house was built.

The station was automated in 1933 and was one of the first in New England to be unmanned. The Fresnel lens was later removed and put on display in the Coast Guard Station at Boothbay Harbor. The lighthouse is not open to the public, and the island is accessible only by private boat and only with permission from the U.S. Fish and Wildlife Service. It is now a wildlife refuge. The lighthouse tower is cared for by a nonprofit group called Franklin Light Preservation.

Franklin Island Light, Muscongus Bay, Me.

An 1890s postcard provides a glimpse of the rambling house and barn complex that once adjoined Franklin Island Lighthouse. The remote station was automated during the 1930s, and all the buildings except the tower and oil house were torn down. The tower is now part of a wildlife refuge. *Photograph from Jeremy D'Entremont's collection*

# Goat Island Lighthouse
## KENNEBUNKPORT

Established in 1835, the diminutive 20-foot-tall stone lighthouse exhibited a Lewis light and was connected to a keeper's dwelling via a long covered walkway. It stood on a tiny islet at Cape Porpoise, near the mouth of the Kennebunk River. The cape was named in 1615 by Captain John Smith for the many porpoises he observed in the waters there.

The station was rebuilt in 1859. The new brick tower was 25 feet tall—not much taller than its predecessor—and exhibited a fifth-order Fresnel lens. A fogbell also stood on the grounds. Later updates included a boathouse in 1905 and an oil house in 1907. In 1978, a strong winter storm destroyed the covered walkway between the tower and the house.

**FOR MORE INFORMATION**
Kennebunkport Conservation Trust
P.O. Box 7028
Cape Porpoise, Maine 04014
www.thekennebunkportconserv ationtrust.org
info@thekennebunkportconserv ationtrust.org

**DIRECTIONS**
See www.lighthousefriends.com /light.asp?ID=551 for directions to the pier at Cape Porpoise.

In 1990, the lighthouse became the last Maine lighthouse to be automated. The light was manned for as long as it was because local residents wanted to ensure the tower would not suffer from vandalism. Following automation, the lighthouse was used by Secret Service personnel keeping watch over President George H. W. Bush, whose family estate is nearby. The fogbell was moved to the grounds of the Kennebunkport Historical Society.

Since 1998, the Kennebunkport Conservation Trust has placed caretakers on-site. The lighthouse is not open to the public except by special arrangement. It can be seen only by private boat or by some area sightseeing cruises. It also can be seen from a pier at Cape Porpoise.

Maine lighthouses were known for the covered walkways that connected the towers to their keepers' quarters. Goat Island Light at Cape Porpoise had one of the longest walkways, as shown in a 1911 collectors' card.
*Photograph from the author's collection*

# Goose Rocks Lighthouse
## NORTH HAVEN

The 51-foot cast-iron, caisson-style lighthouse was constructed in 1890 to mark the eastern entrance to Fox Islands Thorofare. This busy sea lane ran between Vinalhaven and North Haven and was riddled with islands. The three-tier tower had a kerosene-fueled fourth-order Fresnel lens and was painted with a brown daymark. The caisson was filled with concrete and was surrounded by stone riprap to protect it.

By 1963, when the lighthouse was automated, its daymark had been changed to white. With automation came the removal of the classical lens and also concern about the area's notorious fog. For a time, a local lamplighter was paid to row to the station periodically to check the fog signal. The light was solarized with the installation of solar-powered batteries in recent years.

In 2005, the lighthouse was identified for transfer of ownership under the National Historic Lighthouse Preservation Act of 2000. Only one application was made, and it was rejected. The property was then sold by sealed bid to Beacon Preservation of Ansonia, Connecticut. It is not open or accessible to the public and can be seen only by private boat.

Nine solar panels on the middle lantern gallery of Goose Rocks Lighthouse are angled to catch the sun's rays and convert its energy to electricity for the beacon. Two red panels with a narrow white sector are mounted outside the lantern windows to warn ships when they stray from the channel into Little Thorofare. *Photograph by Sue Lott*

# Great Duck Island Lighthouse
## FRENCHBORO

The 42-foot brick lighthouse was built in 1890 to guide ships into Blue Hill Bay. It exhibited a fifth-order lens and had a 1,200-pound fogbell. Behind the tower were three dwellings for the keepers. Only one dwelling remains today. In 1902, the lens was increased to a fourth-order. Also about this time, a tramway was built between the tower and the dwellings to facilitate moving fuel and supplies from the landing to the station.

**FOR MORE INFORMATION**
College of the Atlantic
105 Eden Street
Bar Harbor, ME 04609
207.288.5015
www.coa.edu/irc/gdi.html

The lighthouse was automated in 1986, and the lens was replaced by a modern optic. In 1998, the Coast Guard gave the property to the College of the Atlantic to research the large population of seabirds that live on the island. The lighthouse is not open to the public and can be seen only by boat.

The sprawling multiplex of buildings that comprised Great Duck Island Light Station in 1950 included three keeper's homes, a brick fog signal building, several sheds for storage and tools, and the lighthouse. Water and fuel pipes snaked from the quarters to the sea, while a lone tree struggled to survive between the tower and the little oil house. *Photograph from the Coast Guard Archives*

# Grindle Point Lighthouse
## ISLESBORO

**FOR MORE INFORMATION**
Town of Islesboro
P.O. Box 76
Islesboro, ME 04848
207.734.2253

**DIRECTIONS**
From coastal US 1 at
Lincolnville, take the ferry to
Grindle Point. The lighthouse
is a short walk from the slip.

The island of Islesboro sits in Penobscot Bay. The lighthouse, built in 1851 on land bought from Frances Grindel, guided the region's commercial shipping fleet. The 28-foot tower quickly deteriorated and was replaced in 1874 by a 39-foot brick lighthouse exhibiting a fifth-order lens. The dwelling was attached to the tower by a covered walkway.

By 1934, the beacon was unnecessary and the station was decommissioned. The town of Islesboro bought the property for $1,200, and established the Sailor's Memorial Museum in the keeper's quarters. The station has been well maintained over the years. The town and the Coast Guard relit the beacon in 1987, and it remains active today. The museum is open every day but Monday during the summer months.

A modern flashing green beacon, operated by solar power, seems dwarfed by the spacious lantern of Grindle Point Light in this 2003 photo. The Islesboro lighthouse has been a museum since the 1930s. *Photograph by Sue Lott*

# Halfway Rock Lighthouse
## SOUTH HARPSWELL

A beacon for Casco Bay, the 76-foot granite lighthouse was built on a two-acre islet in 1871 at a cost of $60,000. It exhibited a third-order lens with alternating white and red flashes. The name of the light signified its position halfway between Cape Elizabeth and Cape Small. A half-ton fogbell was bolted to the rock below the tower in 1887. It was replaced in 1905 by a steam fog signal.

FOR MORE INFORMATION
American Lighthouse Foundation
P.O. Box 889
Wells, ME 04090
207.646.0245
www.lighthousefoundation.org

The lighthouse was automated in 1975. The beacon was modernized, and the Fresnel lens was shipped to the Coast Guard Academy in New London, Connecticut, for display. Storms have destroyed all the buildings except the tower. The American Lighthouse Foundation was licensed to maintain the property in 2000 and hopes to restore the lighthouse. It is not open to the public and can be seen only by boat.

Rugged and wave-battered, Halfway Rock Lighthouse is a massive monolith of dovetailed granite blocks perched on a two-acre ledge in Casco Bay. Duty on the offshore tower was challenging. George A. Toothaker, who tended the light from 1872 until 1885, commented to a newspaper reporter of the day: "Me, it affected mentally. Others it affects physically, and I have known of one case where it has driven a man insane . . . Asleep or awake, the beacon haunts you." *Photograph by Jeremy D'Entremont*

# Hendricks Head Lighthouse
## WEST SOUTHPORT

**DIRECTIONS**
From US 1 east of Wiscasset, take ME 27 to West Southport. Follow signs for Beach Road and distant views of the lighthouse. Sightseeing cruises departing from Boothbay Harbor and Bath offer better views.

The sentinel was first lighted in 1829 to mark the entrance to the Sheepscot River. It was a cottage-style design, with the wooden lantern rising from the roof of a granite dwelling. In 1855, it was fitted with a fourth-order Fresnel lens.

The current 39-foot square brick lighthouse replaced the original tower in 1875. A covered walkway led from the dwelling to the tower. For several years, a handbell was used to signal in the fog; in 1891, a fogbell was added, and another covered walkway was built from the house to the pyramidal bell tower. An oil house was built in 1895 after kerosene became the fuel used in the lamp.

The station was decommissioned in 1933 and sold to private owners. With an increase in local boating traffic, the lighthouse was relit in 1951. It remains in private hands and is off-limits to the public. It can be seen from a nearby beach.

A number of lightkeepers were war veterans, having received their appointments as a form of propitiation for injuries incurred while serving their country. Jaruel Marr was assigned to Hendricks Head Lighthouse following his service in the Civil War. Though his sentinel was small, it endured occasional horrendous storms. He recorded one gale that rolled a boulder the size of a modern-day car more than 20 feet. *Photograph by Shirin Pagels*

# Heron Neck Lighthouse
## VINALHAVEN

Built on Greens Island in 1854, the 30-foot brick lighthouse marked the entrance to Hurricane Sound and the fishing community at Carver's Harbor. It abutted a brick dwelling and was equipped with a fifth-order red beacon. A fogbell completed the station but was later upstaged by a fog siren.

In 1895, the leaky dwelling was rebuilt and attached to the old tower, which was still in good condition. An oil house was added to the station in 1903. The lighthouse was automated in 1982, and the lens was replaced by a modern beacon. Seven years later, a fire badly damaged the keeper's dwelling.

The property has been given to the Island Institute. A private individual fronted $200,000 to restore the house. The station is not open to the public and is best viewed by boat.

**FOR MORE INFORMATION**
Island Institute
386 Main Street
Rockland, ME 04841
207.594.9209
www.islandinstitute.org
inquiry@islandinstitute.org

Heron Neck Lighthouse was famous in the early twentieth century for two "fog dogs" named Nemo and Rover, pets of the lightkeepers. The dogs were trained to bark during fogs to warn ships away from the ledges around Green Island. *Photograph by Jeremy D'Entremont*

# Indian Island Lighthouse
## ROCKPORT

**DIRECTIONS**

In Rockport at the intersection of US 1 and ME 90, turn east on West Street, then left on Pascal Avenue. Take Andre Street to Rockport Marine Park. The lighthouse is visible offshore.

Marking the entrance to the harbor at Rockport, the light was established in 1850 as a lantern atop a dwelling. It was equipped with a fourth-order lens in 1856. For unknown reasons, Indian Island Lighthouse was dark for a time beginning in 1859. The station was rebuilt in 1875 as a square brick tower attached to a dwelling. An oil house was added in 1904.

The lighthouse served until 1934, at which time its duties were passed to a small skeleton beacon on Lowell Rock. The property was then sold and remains in private hands. It is not open to the public and is best seen by boat. Rockport offers distant views of the lighthouse.

Bright against a backdrop of green pines, Indian Island Lighthouse has been privately owned since the 1930s. In its heyday during the late nineteenth century, no trees grew on the island. They had been cut down by the early lightkeepers for fuel to help stave off the cold Maine winters. *Photograph by Sue Lott*

# Isle au Haut Lighthouse
## ISLE AU HAUT

Named for its rapid rise in elevation to 556 feet, the island sits in the lower Penobscot Bay. Its lighthouse went into service in 1907. The 40-foot brick tower sat on a granite base and was connected to a spacious house by a wooden walkway. It was equipped with a fourth-order lens. An oil house and storage building completed the station.

In 1934, the station was decommissioned and sold to a private owner. It passed into new hands in 1986 and was converted into a charming bed and breakfast inn without electricity or other modern fixtures. The lighthouse, which was transferred to the town of Isle Au Haut in 1998, was refurbished in 1999. The island is accessed by ferry from Stonington from mid-June through mid-September.

**FOR MORE INFORMATION**
The Keepers House
P.O. Box 26
Isle Au Haut, ME 04645
207.367.2261
www.keepershouse.com

**DIRECTIONS**
From US 1 in Orland, take ME 15 to Stonington and then turn left on Sea Breeze Avenue and continue to the ferry slip.

A glimpse of old-time Maine awaits visitors to Isle au Haut Lighthouse. The sentinel still operates, but the keeper's house has been converted to a cozy bed and breakfast. There is no electricity or telephone, and the innkeepers use a wood stove for cooking and heating. *Photograph by Jeff Burke*

# Kennebec River Light Station
## ARROWSIC

**FOR MORE INFORMATION**
The Range Light Keepers
79 Iron Mine Road
Arrowsic, ME 04530
207.442.7443
For more information on
Friends of Doubling Point Light,
go to www.doublingpoint.org.
The website offers detailed
driving directions to the
lighthouse. The grounds are
open, and there is a small
parking area available.

*Photograph by Shirin Pagels*

Three beacons aid ships through the tricky upper Kennebec River Channel. The diminutive Doubling Point Range Lights were built in 1898 to mark the southern bend in a hazardous double turn in the river. Doubling Point Light, farther north, guides vessels through a second bend.

I n 1898, the Lighthouse Board established a set of range lights along the Kennebec River at Doubling Point.

The two octagonal wooden towers stood 235 yards apart, exhibited fifth-order Fresnel lenses, and were connected by a wooden walkway. The front light was 13 feet tall and stood at water level. The rear light, elevated on the bank, stood at 21 feet above water level. The lights' beams, when lined up one atop the other, guided ships through the tricky river channel.

In 1898, the 23-foot wooden Doubling Point Light was built at the upper end of Fiddler Reach. It exhibited a fourth-order Fresnel lens and guided vessels on the final leg to the port of Bath.

A spacious Victorian-style wooden keeper's house stood near the range lights, along with a fogbell and a tool shed. An oil house was added in 1906. A separate keeper's residence was built at Doubling Point, and it also had a fogbell and an oil house.

In 1979, the Doubling Point Range Lights were automated with modern plastic optics. Soon after, the range lights, Perkins Island, and Squirrel Point became part of Kennebec River Light Station. They were maintained by Karen McLean, the Coast Guard's first female lightkeeper.

*Photograph by Sue Lott*

# THE MAINE LIGHTHOUSE MUSEUM

Maine Lighthouse Museum docents quip that Ken Black was "a beacon of knowledge about lighthouses." Black, a retired Coast Guard officer and founder of the museum, was proud of the visitor-friendly exhibits it offers. (**Right:** *Photograph by Sue Lott*) Children enjoy climbing inside lenses, working block and tackle equipment, and sounding foghorns. (**Left:** *Photograph by Sue Lott*)

It seems only fitting that Maine, with more than seventy lighthouses still standing on its shores, should have a lighthouse museum. When most of us think of lighthouses, we first think of Maine and its fog-afflicted, storm-tossed, rocky coast.

The idea for a museum began in the 1960s when Coast Guard officer Kenneth Black, better known as "Mr. Lighthouse," was in charge of the Coast Guard base in Rockland. Automation of lighthouses was in full swing at the time. Lenses and fogbells were removed, tools and outdated equipment were warehoused, documents were scattered and in danger of being lost.

Black collected and stored as many relics as he could find. When the display spilled out of the Coast Guard base, it went to the Grand Army of the Republic hall in Rockland. Black retired from the Coast Guard in 1971 and became the curator of the collection. It was called the Shore Village Museum after an early name for Rockland. Black continued accumulating artifacts and published a quarterly newsletter, which he always signed off with his personal signature and an earnest reminder to "be neighborly."

By 2005 the museum was drawing thousands of visitors annually and had outgrown its space. The collection was moved to a new building and re-named the Maine Lighthouse Museum. Black was made an honorary member of the board of directors. He has received numerous awards for his work, including a lifetime achievement award from the American Lighthouse Foundation and a Meritorious Service Award from the Coast Guard.

The museum's crowd-pleaser is its large collection of lighthouse lenses. Black called it "visitor-friendly" and a fun place for kids. It is open Monday through Friday from 9:00 A.M. until 5:00 P.M. and on weekends 10:00 A.M. until 5:00 P.M. It is closed Sundays between Columbus Day and Memorial Day.

For more information:
Maine Lighthouse Museum
One Park Drive
P.O. Box F
Rockland, ME 04841
207.594.3301
info@mainelighthousemuseum.com
www.mainelighthousemuseum.com

# Libby Island Lighthouse
## MACHIASPORT

**FOR MORE INFORMATION**
Maine Coastal Island National
Wildlife Refuge
www.fws.gov/northeast/
mainecoastal/

The lighthouse was built sometime between 1822 and 1824 to mark the eastern entrance to Machias Bay. It replaced a crude wooden beacon erected a few years earlier. The 42-foot granite tower exhibited oil lamps and reflectors and included a fogbell. A brick residence was also constructed.

During the 1850s, a fourth-order Fresnel lens was installed. Due to tenacious fogs in the area, the fogbell was replaced by a fog trumpet in 1884. Later the trumpet surrendered its duties to a modern electric horn. The lens was removed and replaced by a modern optic in 1974, at which time the station was automated. All buildings except the tower and foghouse are gone.

The lighthouse was refurbished and solarized in 2000 by the Coast Guard before being transferred to the U.S. Fish and Wildlife Service. It is not open to the public and can be seen only by boat.

Libby Island Light was one of Maine's more remote stations and also one of its foggiest. Various types of bells and horns provided fog warnings over the years. The clamoring signals sounded an average of seventy days a year. *Photograph from the Coast Guard Archives*

# Little River Lighthouse
## CUTLER

Built in 1847 on Little River Island, the lighthouse marked the entrance to Cutler Harbor near the Canadian border. The stone tower was joined to a keeper's house and exhibited oil lamps and reflectors, which were replaced in 1855 by a fifth-order Fresnel lens. The lighthouse was rebuilt in 1876. The new 41-foot cast-iron tower stood apart from the original dwelling. A fogbell also was added at this time. The keeper's house was rebuilt in 1888.

**FOR MORE INFORMATION**
American Lighthouse
Foundation
P.O. Box 889
Wells, ME 04090
207.646.0245
www.lighthousefoundation.org

For most of its career, the tower was white, but circa 1900 it exhibited a brown daymark. In 1960, the U.S. Navy erected two communication towers on the island. The lighthouse was automated in 1975, and the lens was removed five years later when the beacon was relocated to a skeleton tower.

Ownership of the station was transferred to the American Lighthouse Foundation in 2002, and much restoration work has been completed, including relighting the tower. The lighthouse is not yet open to the public and can be seen only by boat. The American Lighthouse Foundation plans to open the house for overnight stays by 2008.

Evidence of a small farm can be seen in this image of the first Little River Lighthouse, circa 1865. Lightkeepers often kept chickens and a cow, and usually planted a garden. The stone house and tower were replaced in 1876 by a 41-foot-tall cast-iron tower. *Photograph from the Coast Guard Archives*

# Lubec Channel Lighthouse
## LUBEC

**DIRECTIONS**
From US 1 in Whiting, take
ME 189 toward the town
of Lubec. Turn right on South
Lubec Road, from which there
are views of the lighthouse.

Lubec had a thriving sardine fishery during the late nineteenth century. The 40-foot sparkplug-style caisson lighthouse was built in 1890 to mark the western entrance to the Lubec Harbor shipping channel. The original sentinel cost $20,000. It exhibited a fifth-order, kerosene-fueled Fresnel lens and had a half-ton fogbell. The lighthouse was classed as a stag station, where only men could serve. To add a small measure of decoration, the architect designed miniature cast-iron lighthouses for the lantern-gallery railing. Over the years, these have all been removed.

The beacon was automated circa 1940. It developed a tilt as its foundation settled, so in 1989 the Coast Guard announced plans to decommission the lighthouse. Local residents protested and managed to arrange a $700,000 renovation that included a reduction of the tower's cant. It continues in service, though it is not open to the public. It can be seen from shore.

Lubec Channel Light typifies the squat, tiered design mariners nicknamed the sparkplug lighthouse. A kinder appellation is wedding-cake light. *Photograph by Jeremy D'Entremont*

# Marshall Point Lighthouse
## St. George

Standing at the entrance to Port Clyde Harbor, a 20-foot stone lighthouse was placed in service in 1832 to assist vessels in the granite, timber, and fishing trades. It exhibited seven lard-oil lamps with reflectors. A stone house abutted the tower.

In 1857, the station was renewed with the construction of a 31-foot brick tower on a granite base. A fifth-order fixed lens was installed. A half-ton bell gave fog warnings. In 1895, lightning struck the dwelling and it had to be rebuilt. Another bolt of sorts came in 1935, when electricity was installed.

The station was automated in 1971, and a modern optic replaced the old lens. The St. George Historical Society refurbished the house in 1990 and set up a museum inside. The station was given to the town of St. George in 1998. The grounds are public, and the museum is open May through October. Caretakers occupy a second-floor apartment.

**FOR MORE INFORMATION**
Marshall Point Lighthouse Museum
P.O. Box 247
Port Clyde, ME 04855
207.372.6450
www.marshallpoint.org

**DIRECTIONS**
From US 1 east of Thomaston, take ME 131 to Port Clyde. Turn left on Drift Inn Road and then turn right on Marshall Point Road. There is parking at the lighthouse.

Glowing through a summer evening fog, the beacon of Marshall Point Light guides ships into Port Clyde Harbor. The old fogbell, now on display, served from 1898 until 1969, when an electric horn replaced it. The small stone tower was built in 1857. During its early years, a covered walkway provided access. *Photograph by Elinor De Wire*

# Matinicus Rock Lighthouse
## MATINICUS

The 32-acre island, which derives its name from a Native American word, sits 18 miles offshore in Penobscot Bay. Twin wooden light towers attached to a central dwelling were built in 1827. The island was isolated and often beset by stormy weather. In 1839, the sea tore down the lights. The beacon was reestablished on a mast until a new dwelling and towers could be rebuilt in 1848.

A one-ton fogbell went into service in 1855. Two years later, the station was rebuilt again, this time with a granite dwelling flanked by granite towers 180 feet apart. The lamps and reflectors were augmented by third-order Fresnel lenses. In 1883, the north light was discontinued to save money, but it was relit in 1888 after mariners complained. In 1923, the light was permanently extinguished.

The Coast Guard automated the south light in 1983. Today the station is owned by the U.S. Fish and Wildlife Service. The dwelling is used for seabird studies. It is not open to the public and can be seen only by boat.

MATINICUS ROCK LIGHT

"A confused pile of loose stone" is how the U.S. Lighthouse Board described Matinicus Rock in an 1891 report. The station's twin lights were designed to circumvent confusion with neighboring beacons in the Gulf of Maine. A 1910 collectors' card gave the place a pleasant appearance, but it had a reputation for fierce storms and extreme isolation. *Photograph from the author's collection*

# Monhegan Island Lighthouse
## MONHEGAN

The island, 10 miles offshore on the approach to Muscongus Bay, was marked with a beacon in 1824. The granite tower, which was flanked by a wooden dwelling, stood on the island's highest point. It exhibited ten Lewis lamps and reflectors. The tower soon began to deteriorate and was rebuilt in 1850. A fogbell was installed in 1854. The 47-foot granite sentinel was fitted with a second-order Fresnel lens in 1856. A new 2-story dwelling was constructed in 1874, making room for two keepers.

About this time, the fogbell was discontinued and a fog trumpet was installed on nearby Manana Island. It proved insufficient, so a whistle was added at Monhegan Island Lighthouse. The keeper at the lighthouse operated both signals.

The 1857 residence was razed in 1922, leaving one dwelling. The light was automated in 1959, and three years later the residence was sold. The property was transferred to the Monhegan Historical and Cultural Museum in 1997, and they rebuilt the original dwelling to house a museum.

**FOR MORE INFORMATION**
Monhegan Museum
1 Lighthouse Hill
Monhegan, ME 04852
207.596.7003
www.monheganmuseum.org
museum@monheganmuseum.org

**HOURS OF OPERATION**
Open daily July through September from 11:30 A.M. to 3:30 P.M.

**DIRECTIONS**
Take the ferry from Port Clyde, New Harbor, or Boothbay Harbor to Monhegan Island. Take Wharf Hill Road to Main Street and turn left to Lighthouse Hill Road. Hike uphill to the lighthouse about a half mile.

Monhegan Island, meaning "island of the sea" in Abenaki, lies 10 miles off the coast of Maine. This image from the book *All Among the Lighthouses* portrays the idyllic site during the early 1880s. *Photograph from the author's collection*

# Moose Peak Lighthouse
## JONESPORT

Located on foggy Mistake Island, five miles offshore, this lighthouse served shipping on the southwest side of the entrance to Main Channel Way. It was commissioned in 1827 at a cost of $4,000 and then rebuilt in 1851. The 57-foot brick tower was renovated and fitted with a second-order Fresnel lens in 1856. A new residence was built in 1903.

Fog signaling was an important part of the station's mission, since fog envelops the region about 20 percent of the time. The foghorn averaged 1,600 hours of operation and once ran for 181 consecutive hours during the summer of 1916.

The lighthouse was automated in 1972, and the lens was replaced by a modern optic. It was solarized in 1999. The 1903 house was destroyed in 1982 when a military ordinance training team used it as a target. The lighthouse is not open to the public. The island is managed by the Nature Conservancy. The grounds can be accessed by boat, but visitors must remain on designated trails.

Moose Peak Light Station, off Jonesport, once boasted numerous buildings, including a granite light tower connected to a spacious Victorian house via a covered walkway. The house was condemned in 1982 and later destroyed in a military exercise. Only the tower and oil house remain today. *Photograph from the author's collection*

# Mount Desert Rock Lighthouse
## FRENCHBORO

The sea-swept rock beneath this lighthouse, 26 miles south of Mount Desert Island, has had a lighthouse since 1830 to guide shipping into Frenchman Bay and Blue Hill Bay. The wooden tower stood at one end of a stone dwelling and exhibited eight lamps with reflectors. The storm-battered sentinel was replaced in 1847 by a 58-foot granite lighthouse with two dwellings. It was upgraded with a fogbell and a third-order Fresnel lens in 1858. The stone house continued in service until 1876, at which time it was replaced. A third keeper's dwelling was built in 1893, and a walkway connected the homes with the tower.

**FOR MORE INFORMATION**
College of the Atlantic
105 Eden Street
Bar Harbor, ME 04609
207.288.5015
www.coa.edu/html/
mountdesertrock.htm

The fogbell was replaced with a whistle in 1889. By this time, three lightkeepers and their families lived on the rock. In 1931, generators were installed for electricity.

Storms damaged the station over the years. One gale tore out the walkway and swept away fuel tanks. In the mid-1970s, the lantern was removed so that an exposed aerobeacon could be installed. After a flurry of complaints, the lantern was put back in 1985.

The station is owned by the College of the Atlantic, which conducts marine studies from the island. The group has restored some of the buildings. The lighthouse is not open to the public and can be seen only by boat.

One of New England's most challenging light stations was located on Mount Desert Rock. A nineteenth-century artist romanticized the place (**Left:** *Photograph from the National Archives*), adding fishermen and a nearby island, but it was really a far-flung and desolate assignment miles from shore. There was no soil at the site, so lighthouse families hauled dirt, packed it in the rock crevices, and planted vegetables and flowers. The gardens added color to an otherwise gray world of rocks, tower, and sea. (**Right:** *Photograph from the Coast Guard Archives*)

# Narraguagus Lighthouse
## MILBRIDGE

**FOR MORE INFORMATION**
See
www.robertsonseatours.com
for cruise information.

To meet the needs of lumber vessels traveling in and out of the Narraguagus River, a light was established on Pond Island in 1853. The first tower rose from the roof of the keeper's house. It was redesigned in 1875 with a new wood-frame house surrounding a 31-foot granite tower. A few years later, one end of the house was taken down, leaving most of the exterior of the conical tower visible and connected to a brick workroom. The station operated a fifth-order Fresnel lens for most of its career.

The beacon was abandoned in 1934, and the property was sold to private owners. It remains in private hands and is not open to the public. The lighthouse is best seen by boat. A cruise from Milbridge provides a good view.

Lightkeepers were known for their solicitude. In August 1929, the Canadian schooner *Valdare* wrecked near Narraguagus Lighthouse, shown in this recent image. Keeper Charles Tracey took in the rescued crew and cared for them for twelve days until they were well enough to leave. *Photograph by Kraig Anderson*

# Nash Island Lighthouse
## ADDISON

This lighthouse was erected in 1838 to mark the entrance to the Pleasant River. The area was a thriving shipbuilding and export center. A pair of islands lay several miles off Cape Split, and a beacon was established on the smaller of the two. A short stone tower was joined to a wood-frame house by means of a

**FOR MORE INFORMATION**
Friends of Nash Island Light
P.O. Box 250
Addison, ME 04606

covered walkway. Oil lamps and reflectors served until 1856, at which time a fourth-order Fresnel lens went into service.

In 1873, a new 51-foot square brick tower was built, and the lens was transferred to the new tower. A fogbell and bell house were added in 1888. At this time, three keepers lived at the station. The station was automated in 1958, and all buildings were razed except the tower and adjoining workroom. The light was extinguished in 1982. A nonprofit group is working to restore the tower.

A lightkeeper, his wife, and their pets—a dog and a caged parrot—posed for a photo at Nash Island Lighthouse circa 1880. The station became obsolete during the 1940s, and every building but the tower was torn down. Today the island is a wildlife refuge. *Photograph from the Coast Guard Archives*

# Owls Head Lighthouse
## OWLS HEAD

**FOR MORE INFORMATION**
Owls Head Light State Park
Owls Head, ME 04854
207.941.4014

**DIRECTIONS**
From Rockland, take ME 73 south and turn left on North Shore Drive. In Owls Head, turn left on Main Street. Take another left onto Lighthouse Road. There is a parking area near the lighthouse.

Lime quarries brought shipping to Rockland in the early nineteenth century and necessitated construction of a lighthouse at the entrance to the harbor. Owls Head Light was built in 1825 on a high promontory that some believe resembles the head of an owl. The 30-foot brick tower exhibited oil lamps and reflectors until 1856, at which time a fourth-order lens was installed. A wood-frame house sat below the tower in a protected area of trees and was connected to the tower by a wooden ramp and stairs. The station also had a fogbell. An oil house was added in 1895.

The light was automated in 1989, but the lens remained in place. An electric foghorn has replaced the old bell. The lighthouse and the keeper's house currently are occupied by a Coast Guard family and are not open to the public, but the grounds are open as part of a state park.

This small sentry offering guidance to ships entering Rockland Harbor is perched atop a high promontory called Owls Head. (**Left:** *Photograph by Yvonne Zemotel*).
The light station is plagued by fog. During the 1930s, a lightkeeper trained his dog to ring the fogbell by yanking on a rope tied to the clapper. A collectors' card featured a stylized version of the bell hanging in a wooden tower.
(**Right:** *Photograph from the author's collection*)

# Pemaquid Point Lighthouse
## BRISTOL

The stone lighthouse was constructed on a picturesque rocky point in 1827 to mark the entrance to Muscongus Bay and John Bay. Reports indicate salt water was used in the mortar, which led to the tower's quick deterioration. A new 35-foot stone lighthouse was built in 1835, attached to a sturdy house and a workroom. It held ten lamps and reflectors. These were improved with the installation of a fourth-order Fresnel lens in 1856. A year later, the dwelling was replaced with a wood-frame house.

A fogbell and bell house were added in 1897. Lightkeepers manually operated the bell for a year before an automatic bell striker was installed to take over the work. By 1934, the station was automated, and the house stood empty. A park was established on the point, and the house was opened as the Fishermen's Museum in 1972. The grounds and museum are maintained by the town of Bristol. The tower itself is well maintained by a chapter of the American Lighthouse Foundation.

**FOR MORE INFORMATION**
Friends of Pemaquid Point
Lighthouse
P.O. Box 353
Bristol, ME 04539
backlog@tidewater.net

The Fishermen's Museum
Pemaquid Point Road
New Harbor, ME 04554
207.677.2494

**HOURS OF OPERATION**
The tower is open for tours daily Memorial Day through Columbus Day from 1:00 P.M. to 5:00 P.M. The museum is open daily during summer.

**DIRECTIONS**
From US 1 in Damariscotta, take ME 130 to Bristol. The road terminates at the lighthouse parking area.

Striated rocks bear witness to the unforgiving shore surrounding Pemaquid Point Lighthouse at Bristol. The station is touted as Maine's prettiest. *Photograph by Sue Lott*

# Perkins Island Lighthouse
## GEORGETOWN

**FOR MORE INFORMATION**
Friends of Perkins Island
Lighthouse
P.O. Box 376
Georgetown, ME 04548
perkinslight@hotmail.com

The quaint 23-foot wooden lighthouse was built in 1898 as a guide for the Kennebec River. It stood on an island near the entrance to the river. The lantern exhibited a fifth-order lens. The station also included a two-story dwelling and a barn. A boathouse and half-ton fogbell were added in 1902, and a brick oil house was constructed in 1906.

The station was automated in 1959. In 1979, the lens was removed in favor of a modern optic. The old fogbell went to the grounds of the Georgetown High School, but the bell tower remained and was restored in 2000. A chapter of the American Lighthouse Foundation is raising money to restore the house and the tower. The station is not open to the public and is best viewed by boat.

Hints of former beauty can be seen in the rambling house, quaint light, and pyramidal fogbell tower at Perkins Island. The bell tower was restored in 2000, but the house awaits a much-needed makeover. The tower is licensed to the American Lighthouse Foundation. *Photograph by Sue Lott*

# Petit Manan Lighthouse
## MILBRIDGE

The original lighthouse and dwelling were rubble stone. The 25-foot-tall tower was built in 1817 on a treeless island 14 miles off Bar Harbor to warn of a sandbar and to guide vessels into several small bays. The little sentinel deteriorated and was replaced in 1854 by a much taller 119-foot granite tower. It was fitted with a second-order Fresnel lens and a fogbell.

The lighthouse was damaged in storms in 1856 and in 1869. The 1869 storm caused the weights that turned the lens to crash down through the tower, taking out some of the stairway. Repairs were made, and the tower was strengthened with vertical tie rods. Due to heavy fog in the area, in 1869 the fogbell was replaced with a steam whistle.

The light was electrified in 1938 and was automated in 1972. A modern optic replaced the classical Fresnel lens. The lens was moved to the Shore Village Museum (now the Maine Lighthouse Museum), and the fogbell went to the grounds of a Milbridge school. The lighthouse is part of Maine Coastal Islands National Wildlife Refuge. Researchers live in the keeper's house and use the tower to observe wildlife. The station is not open to the public and is best seen by boat.

FOR MORE INFORMATION
Maine Coastal Islands National Wildlife Refuge
www.fws.gov/northeast/mainecoastal/

THE PETIT MANAN LIGHTHOUSE, MAINE
A granite tower

Three uniformed lightkeepers and their families stood for a portrait at Petit Manan Lighthouse during the 1890s. The tall granite tower was anything but petite. Its 119-foot-high pinnacle attracted lightning and birds but stood firm during powerful storms. *Photograph from Coast Guard Museum Northwest*

# Pond Island Lighthouse
## POPHAM BEACH

A stone sentinel was built on the 10-acre island in 1821 to mark the entrance to the Kennebec River. It supplemented the light at Seguin Island. Lamps and reflectors served as a beacon. In 1855, the crumbling tower was replaced by a 20-foot brick lighthouse with a new fifth-order lens. The tower was joined to a wood-frame house by a short, covered walkway. There also was a fogbell at the station.

The light was automated in 1963 with a modern optic and was later solarized. The Coast Guard razed the house and other buildings. The U.S. Fish and Wildlife Service currently manages the island. The lighthouse is not open to the public and is best viewed by boat.

Bereft of its keeper's house and other auxiliary buildings, Pond Island Light stands a lonely watch on Pond Island National Wildlife Refuge. The tower's Fresnel lens was replaced by a modern solarized beacon in recent years. *Photograph by Jeremy D'Entremont*

# Portland Breakwater Lighthouse
## SOUTH PORTLAND

Established in 1855, the lighthouse sat at the end of an 1,800-foot-long stone breakwater designed to protect the harbor during storms. The wooden tower was octagonal in shape and supported a sixth-order Fresnel lens. The keeper lived ashore and walked the breakwater each day to tend the light.

**DIRECTIONS**
From ME 77 in South Portland, turn left on Broadway and then left on Pickett Street, which becomes Madison Street and ends at Bug Light Park.

When the breakwater was lengthened during the 1870s, a new lighthouse was built. It went into service and quickly earned the nickname Bug Light. The cast-iron tower mimicked a Greek monument. A dwelling was built beside it in 1889, and a small fogbell was added in 1897. In 1934, the keeper of nearby Spring Point Ledge Light took over duties at the breakwater light, and the keeper's dwelling at Portland Breakwater Lighthouse was razed. The light was decommissioned in 1942.

The sentinel was refurbished during the late 1980s and again in 2002, at which time it was relit as an aid to navigation. The tower is cared for by the Rotary Club of South Portland–Cape Elizabeth. A park was established around it. Though the lighthouse is not open to the public, the grounds can be visited as part of Bug Light Park.

Breakwaters usually are marked with lighthouses to guide ships around them, but few sentinels are as elegant as Portland Breakwater Light. It was modeled after the fourth-century Greek choragic monument of Lysicrates and features Corinthian columns.
*Photograph by Shirin Pagels*

# Portland Head Lighthouse
## CAPE ELIZABETH

**FOR MORE INFORMATION**
The Museum at Portland Head
Lighthouse
P.O. Box 252
Cape Elizabeth, ME 04107
207.799.2661
www.portlandheadlight.com

**DIRECTIONS**
From ME 77 in South Portland,
turn left on Broadway and
then right on Cottage Road,
which becomes Shore Road
and leads to the lighthouse in
Fort Williams Park.

Maine's oldest lighthouse was erected in 1791 to mark the entrance to Portland Harbor. At this time, Maine was not yet a state, and our nation's youthful Congress was strapped for money. The tower cost about $1,500, and its first keeper accepted a free house and land to farm as payment. The illuminating apparatus probably consisted of simple lard or whale-oil lamps. A Lewis light replaced these lamps in 1813. The lights were renewed in 1850, but by this time the station was much in need of work.

In 1855, a fourth-order Fresnel lens was installed and a fogbell was added. The wooden stairs in the tower were replaced by cast-iron steps. A decade later, the tower was heightened by 20 feet and upgraded with a second-order light. The tower was lowered by 20 feet in 1883 when a fourth-order lens was installed, but it was then raised and upgraded again a year later. In 1891, a beautiful Victorian residence for the keepers replaced the original stone house.

In 1958, the Fresnel lens was replaced by a modern optic. The station was automated on August 7, 1989, on the bicentennial of the U.S. Lighthouse Establishment. Today the station is a popular museum. Hours vary. Call or check the Museum at Portland Head Lighthouse website.

Holiday wreaths decorate the windows and porch railing of the sprawling Victorian duplex at Portland Head Lighthouse. The station, which includes Maine's oldest and most visited lighthouse, is now a museum.
*Photograph by Yvonne Zemotel*

# Prospect Harbor Lighthouse
## PROSPECT HARBOR

The lighthouse was constructed in 1850 to aid an active fishing fleet in the area. The original granite tower was attached to the dwelling. It began service with lamps and reflectors but was inactive from 1859 to 1870 due to changing shipping needs. The tower then served until 1891, at which time it was replaced by a wooden sentinel and an adjacent wood-frame house.

The new 38-foot lighthouse was equipped with a fifth-order Fresnel lens. A covered walkway originally connected the tower and house, but it was later removed. An oil house was built in 1905 to house flammable kerosene. The beacon was automated in 1934, and the lens was replaced by a modern optic in 1951.

The station sits on a Navy base, where the keeper's quarters now serve as a vacation house for military personnel. The lighthouse, recently renovated, is licensed to the American Lighthouse Foundation.

**FOR MORE INFORMATION**
American Lighthouse Foundation
P.O. Box 889
Wells, ME 04090
207.646.0245

**DIRECTIONS**
From ME 186 north of Prospect Harbor, turn east on ME 195 and then right on Lighthouse Road. The tower can be seen along this road near the gate to the naval base.

The keeper of the first Prospect Harbor Lighthouse posed with his wife and three daughters circa 1885. A shade was drawn around the lens to protect it from harsh sunlight, which could discolor the prisms and dry out the putty holding them in place. *Photograph from the Coast Guard Archives*

# Pumpkin Island Lighthouse
## LITTLE DEER ISLE

**DIRECTIONS**

From US 1 at Orland, take ME 175 to Black Corner. Turn right on ME 15 and drive to Little Deer Isle. Turn right on Eggemoggin Road and drive to the end of the island, where the lighthouse can be seen offshore.

The lighthouse was completed in 1854 in eastern Penobscot Bay to mark Eggemoggin Reach, a busy lumber portal. The 25-foot brick tower was attached to a dwelling and exhibited a fifth-order Fresnel lens. The station also included a boathouse and an oil house. In 1889, the tower was improved with a new lantern that increased its height to 28 feet.

The beacon was decommissioned in 1934, and the property was sold. It remains in private hands. The lighthouse is not open to the public but can be viewed from the mainland or by boat.

The fifth-order lens of Pumpkin Island Light seems dwarfed by its large lantern room in a late-nineteenth-century image. Blocking panels can be seen on one side of the lantern; they prevent the light beams from being seen outside the shipping channel. *Photograph from the National Archives*

# Ram Island Ledge Lighthouse
## BOOTHBAY HARBOR

Fishermen kept a lamp hung on a dory in the passage to the harbor before the lighthouse was built in 1883. The upper part of the 35-foot tower is brick, and the lower part is granite. An open walkway led over the rocks to the dwelling. The lantern exhibited a fourth-order Fresnel lens, and a small fogbell was suspended on the seaward side of the tower.

**FOR MORE INFORMATION**
Ram Island Preservation Society
Box 123
Boothbay, ME 04537
207.633.4727

The lighthouse was automated in 1965. Absence of keepers spelled trouble. The station was vandalized, and the Fresnel lens was stolen. It was later found and placed in the Boothbay Regional Historical Society Museum. Renovations were done in 1977, and the property was transferred to the Grand Banks Schooner Museum Trust in 1998. Caretakers now live in the quarters. They offer tours by special arrangement. The lighthouse is accessed by boat.

Casco Bay's rugged Ram Island Ledge Lighthouse is one of only a few New England sentinels with diagonal astragals, metal frames that hold the lantern windows in place. The bowed panes of glass, developed during the late nineteenth century, allowed rain and snow to slide away easily and interfered less with the light rays than flat panes did. *Photograph by Jeremy D'Entremont*

# Ram Island Lighthouse
## Cape Elizabeth

The island is at the entrance to Portland Harbor and sits amid rock ledges. A daymark in the form of a spindle was placed at the site in 1855. It was replaced by a wooden tripod in 1873. The lighthouse was built in 1905 after several shipwrecks underscored its need. The 90-foot tower was fitted with a third-order kerosene-fueled Fresnel lens and a fogbell. Only men were permitted to live at the lonely water-bound sentinel.

A submarine cable from Portland brought electricity to the station in 1958. It was automated the following year. The Coast Guard recently solarized the beacon. The lighthouse is not open to the public and is best viewed by boat. It can be seen in the distance from Portland Head Lighthouse. It is now licensed to the American Lighthouse Foundation.

Glimpses of everyday life at a Maine lighthouse are evident in this 1890s snapshot of Ram Island Lighthouse. Laundry hangs on a line to dry, tools lie scattered inside a fenced vegetable garden, and visitors lounge on the wooden walkway connecting the house and light tower. *Photograph from the Coast Guard Archives*

# Rockland Breakwater Lighthouse
## ROCKLAND

During construction of a granite breakwater in 1889 at Rockland Harbor, a small wooden beacon was maintained on the structure. It was replaced by a 25-foot brick lighthouse in 1902. The tower was attached to a brick and wood dwelling. A fourth-order Fresnel lens provided the beacon.

The light was automated in 1963, and the lens was removed in favor of a modern optic. Within ten years, the light's usefulness was in doubt, and the Coast Guard announced plans to extinguish the beacon and tear down the lighthouse. Public outcry and an offer by a local resort to maintain the structure resulted in a temporary arrangement to keep it lit.

In 1998, the lighthouse was permanently rescued from destruction under the Maine Lights Program with an ownership transfer to the Rockland City Council. A chapter of the American Lighthouse Foundation cares for it.

**FOR MORE INFORMATION**
Friends of Rockland Breakwater
Lighthouse
P.O. Box 741
Rockland, ME 04841
207.785.4609
www.rocklandlighthouse.com

**HOURS OF OPERATION**
Tours of the tower are offered from 9:00 A.M. to 6:00 P.M. on Saturdays and Sundays from May through October

**DIRECTIONS**
On US 1 North of Rockland, turn right on Waldo Avenue, right on Samoset Road, and then drive to the end. Walk the breakwater to the lighthouse.

A guide for vessels entering Rockland Harbor, the lighthouse on the 0.87-mile-long breakwater is a handsome two-story edifice complete with dormer windows, a square tower adjoining the house, and a deck wrapping around the entire structure. *Photograph from the author's collection*

# Saddleback Ledge Lighthouse
## VINALHAVEN

The lonely, barren rock ledge at the south entrance to East Penobscot Bay received a lighthouse in 1839. Cost for the sentinel was $15,000—expensive at the time but worth the price tag. The ledge is pummeled by severe weather year-round. Keepers at first lived inside the 42-foot conical tower. The only other building on the ledge was a privy. Separate keeper's quarters were built a few years later.

In 1855, the Lewis light was replaced by a fifth-order Fresnel lens. A fogbell was added in 1887. Also about this time an iron derrick with a bosun's chair was built to hoist people safely from the boat landing to the ledge. The lighthouse was automated in 1954, and its lens was replaced by a modern optic. Keepers were relieved, since it was not a pleasant place to serve. The dwelling was torn down circa 1960. The lighthouse is not open to the public and can be seen only by boat.

Perched atop a rock ledge shaped like a horse's saddle, the granite tower of Saddleback Light has stood watch at the southern entrance to East Penobscot Bay since 1839. It was designed by architect Alexander Parris, the talent behind many notable public buildings of the early nineteenth century. *Photograph from the Coast Guard Archives*

# Seguin Island Lighthouse
## POPHAM BEACH

The first sentinel was built in 1795. The wooden tower and dwelling sat at an elevation of more than 100 feet, the highest point of the island, and provided guidance for ships entering the Kennebec River. The origin of the name *Seguin* is said by some to be a corruption of the Native American word *sutquin,* meaning "place where the sea vomits." Others claim that it originates from a Native American word for "hump."

**FOR MORE INFORMATION**
Friends of Seguin Island, Inc.
P.O. Box 866
Bath, ME 04530
www.seguinisland.org

The lighthouse was near collapse in 1819 when it was replaced by a new stone tower and fogbell. The lantern had fifteen oil lamps and reflectors, but the light proved insufficient, and nine more lamps were added during the 1840s. As the shipbuilding and fishing industries grew in nearby Bath, a better light was planned. In 1857, a 53-foot stone tower was built and fitted with a first-order fixed lens. The beacon was the highest in Maine and was visible for more than 20 miles. A fog whistle was installed in 1870, followed by a foghorn a few years later.

The station was automated in 1985. Its opulent lens, the only first-order lens still operational in Maine, was left in place. Ownership of the property was transferred to a nonprofit group. The site is well maintained by caretakers from Memorial Day through Labor Day, during which time the tower, museum, and gift shop are open to the public. The lighthouse is accessible only by boat. Summer cruises are offered by Maine Maritime Museum.

Located a mile off the mouth of the Kennebec River, Seguin Island Lighthouse was a rough assignment. Snakes infested the island, and access was challenged by swift currents and harsh weather. A popular legend holds that one of the station's keepers brought a piano to the station to ease his wife's loneliness and then murdered her because she could play only one song. *Photograph from the author's collection*

# Spring Point Ledge Lighthouse
## SOUTH PORTLAND

**FOR MORE INFORMATION**
Spring Point Ledge
Lighthouse Trust
P.O. Box 2311
South Portland, ME 04106
207.767.7488
www.springpointlight.org

**DIRECTIONS**
From ME 77 in South Portland, turn right on Broadway and then right on Pickett Street. Turn left on Fort Road and drive to the Portland Harbor Museum. From the museum, it's a short but strenuous walk to the lighthouse.

The sparkplug-style caisson lighthouse went into service in 1897 to warn ships off a rock ledge on the west side of the channel into Portland Harbor. The cast-iron tower was 54 feet tall and was equipped with a fifth-order Fresnel lens fueled by kerosene. A fogbell mounted on the gallery was operated by an automatic striker. Only men were permitted to live at the light.

The beacon was electrified in 1934. A granite breakwater was constructed over the ledge and was connected to the lighthouse in 1951. It was automated a few years later with a modern optic and an electric horn. In 1998, ownership of the lighthouse was transferred via the Maine Lights Program to a nonprofit group. Open houses are held several times a year. Contact Spring Point Ledge Lighthouse Trust for dates.

SPRING POINT LEDGE LIGHT

A 1910 collectors' card shows a fogbell hanging from the lantern of South Portland's Spring Point Lighthouse. The black trumpet-shaped protrusion on the right was a light sector box, intended to direct and confine the beams to a specific area of the harbor. *Photograph from the author's collection*

# Squirrel Point Lighthouse
## ARROWSIC

This quaint 25-foot wooden lighthouse was built in 1898 to mark the twisting channel of the Kennebec River. It was fitted with a fifth-order Fresnel lens and a fog signal. Also included at the station were a Victorian-style house and a barn. A boathouse and an oil house were built a few years later.

The station was automated in 1979, and its lens was replaced by a modern optic. The lens eventually went on display at the museum at Portland Head Light. In 1998, the property was deeded to a nonprofit group, but the non-profit was not able to care for the station. The lighthouse deteriorated, and the group put it up for sale. This action violated preservation guidelines. In a lengthy court case, the lighthouse reverted to government ownership.

**DIRECTIONS**
From US 1 east of Bath, take ME 127 and then turn right on Steen Road. Turn left on Bald Head Road and drive to the end. A half-mile path leads to the lighthouse; it can be quite mosquito-infested during summer. The station can also be seen from cruises that depart from Bath and from Boothbay Harbor.

The site will be conveyed to public ownership through the National Historic Lighthouse Preservation Act of 2000. Currently, however, the lighthouse is not open to the public.

Ruby glass window panes on Squirrel Point Lighthouse identify it as a channel beacon. The Kennebec River sentinel serves vessels headed into the shipyard town of Bath. Its red flash lasts three seconds, and a white sector warns ships when they stray from the channel.
*Photograph by Shirin Pagels*

# Tenants Harbor Lighthouse
## TENANTS HARBOR

Built in 1858 on 22-acre Southern Island, the lighthouse marked the entrance to Tenants Harbor. The 27-foot cylindrical brick tower was connected to a wooden dwelling. It exhibited a red, flashing, fourth-order lens. An oil house was added in 1906 after the lens was converted to kerosene.

The sentinel had a short career; it was decommissioned in 1934. The lens was removed, and the property was sold to private owners. It passed through many hands until renowned painter Andrew Wyeth purchased it in 1978. The current owner is Wyeth's son, painter Jamie Wyeth. The lighthouse is not open to the public and is best seen by boat.

Lovely Tenants Harbor Light sits on a grassy knoll on Southern Island overlooking Penobscot Bay. It was decommissioned during the 1930s. Since 1978, it has been owned by the Wyeth family of famous painters. *Photograph by Jeremy D'Entremont*

# Two Bush Island Lighthouse
## SPRUCE HEAD

The light was established in 1897 to guide vessels into Two Bush Channel in Penobscot Bay. The island and channel took their names from two trees that were landmarks for sailors before the lighthouse was built. The 42-foot square brick tower had an attached workroom. A wood-frame dwelling stood nearby.

**FOR MORE INFORMATION**
Maine Coastal Islands National Wildlife Refuge
P.O. Box 279
Milbridge, Maine 04658
207.546.2124

The lighthouse was automated in 1964. The keeper's house was torn down as part of a military exercise in 1970. The Coast Guard solarized the light in recent years, and it continues in service. The island is owned by the U.S. Fish and Wildlife Service. The lighthouse is not open to the public and is best seen by boat.

Two scrubby trees once served as a daymark for ships passing Two Bush Island. Its lighthouse was built in 1897. The tower was surmounted by a workroom and a bell house in this vintage postcard image. The mechanical bell striker is visible on the scaffold to the right. *Photograph by Jeremy D'Entremont*

# West Quoddy Head Lighthouse
## LUBEC

**FOR MORE INFORMATION**
West Quoddy Head Light
Keepers Association
P.O. Box 378
Lubec, ME 04652
207.733.2180
www.westquoddy.com
info@westquoddy.com

**HOURS OF OPERATION**
The grounds are open to the public all year. A visitor center, complete with displays, is open 10:00 AM to 4:00 PM Memorial Day through mid-October.

**DIRECTIONS**
Follow directions for Lubec Channel Light. Continue on South Lubec Road to signs for West Quoddy Head State Park.

This lighthouse was built in 1808 at the easternmost point of the United States. Oil lamps and reflectors provided the beacon. The stone tower had a fog cannon and warned mariners of the treacherous Sail Rocks. In 1820, a hand-operated fogbell was installed. It is considered to be the first lighthouse fogbell in the nation.

In 1858, a new 49-foot brick lighthouse was constructed. It was equipped with a third-order lens and painted in bright red-and-white horizontal stripes. A comfortable new house was built for the keeper. The station was automated in 1988. The fogbell was replaced in 1869 by a fog trumpet. The station was automated in 1988.

Renowned for its candy-stick paint scheme, West Quoddy Light shows up well in fog and winter snow. It is the easternmost lighthouse in the United States and lays claim to receiving the nation's first rays of dawn each day.
*Photograph from the National Oceanic & Atmospheric Administration*

# Whaleback Lighthouse
## KITTERY

A beacon for the entrance to Portsmouth and the Piscataqua River, this lighthouse was originally built in 1831. The stone tower stood on a granite foundation on a ledge of rock that mariners called the Whale's Back. It exhibited a curious pair of piggyback beacons, probably designed to distinguish it from nearby Portsmouth Light. The foundation was poorly constructed but was repaired, and the tower endured storms and pounding waves. A fourth-order Fresnel lens replaced the dual beacons in 1855.

By 1872, the old tower had developed cracks and was in danger of collapse. It was replaced by a 50-foot granite lighthouse. The lens was transferred to the new lantern, and the old tower was razed and replaced by an iron fog-signal building.

The sentinel was automated in 1963, and the lens was replaced by a modern optic. The volume of the foghorns was reduced in 1991 after it was discovered the concussion of the sound was causing damage to the tower masonry.

The lighthouse remains an active aid to navigation and is now licensed to the American Lighthouse Foundation. It is not open to the public. It can be seen in the distance from Portsmouth Harbor Lighthouse and from other shore sites. The closest mainland view is from Fort Foster, a public park in Kittery, Maine. The lighthouse can also be seen from various sightseeing cruises that depart from Portsmouth.

Old and new are seen in this engraving of Kittery's Whaleback Lighthouse. The original tower was used as a staging point for building its taller and sturdier successor in 1872. *Photograph from the author's collection*

# Whitehead Lighthouse
## St. George

**FOR MORE INFORMATION**
Whitehead Lightkeepers
Program
www.pineisland.org/
lightkeepers.htm

This lighthouse marked the western entrance to Muscle Ridge Channel in Penobscot Bay. It was built in 1807 with a wooden octagonal design, at which time it was probably equipped with spider lamps or pan lamps fueled by whale oil. In 1817, a Lewis light was installed. A half-ton fogbell was added to the station in 1830. Fog was such a problem that an experimental tidal fogbell was installed in 1837. Storms ultimately broke the apparatus, and the original system was returned. A whistle replaced the bell in 1869.

A new 41-foot granite lighthouse was built in 1852. It was upgraded with a fourth-order Fresnel lens five years later. Two dwellings were built for the keepers. In 1933, electricity was installed and foghorns replaced the old, hoarse whistle. The beacon was automated during the 1980s with a modern optic and was later solarized. The lens was moved to the Shore Village Museum (now the Maine Lighthouse Museum).

In 1997, the station was given to the Pine Island Camp for kids. Youths currently work to restore and preserve the station. It is not open to the public, but plans are in the works to establish a museum on the island. The lighthouse is best seen by boat.

Whitehead Lighthouse was known for fog and had at least one experimental signal, a tide-actuated bell installed in 1837. Within a few years, storms irreparably damaged the apparatus, and the keeper began operating it with a rope run from the bell clapper to his quarters. He could even operate the bell from his bed. *Photograph from the National Archives*

# Whitlocks Mill Lighthouse
## CALAIS

A lantern hung from a tree by the Whitlock family was the first beacon to mark the St. Croix River. At a critical turning point in the river, it provided guidance to lumber ships plying the port at Calais. In 1910, the makeshift lantern was replaced by 32-foot brick-and-stone lighthouse equipped with a fourth-order lens and a fogbell. The beacon was green, signifying the starboard side of the channel. A spacious, two-story, wood-frame dwelling stood on the hillock behind the tower, along with a rough stone oil house.

**FOR MORE INFORMATION**
St. Croix Historical Society
P.O. Box 242
Calais, ME 04619
207.454.2604
www.stcroixhistorical.org

The light was automated in 1969, and the station was leased for a time to the Washington County Vocational Institute. The keeper's house and other buildings, aside from the lighthouse tower, are privately owned. In 1998, ownership of the lighthouse was transferred via the Maine Lights Program to the St. Croix Historical Society. It was the last lighthouse built in Maine and is the northernmost sentinel in New England. The house is privately owned. The lighthouse is not open to the public and is best seen by boat.

Lilacs and spent dandelions color the spring lawn at Whitlocks Mill Lighthouse. The small sentinel stands watch over the St. Croix River near Calais, at the nation's easternmost border with Canada. *Photograph by Jeremy D'Entremont*

# Winter Harbor Lighthouse
## WINTER HARBOR

**DIRECTIONS**

From US 1 west of West Gouldsboro, take ME 186 south and then turn right on Moore Road. Enter Acadia National Park on one-way Schoodic Road. One mile into the park, the lighthouse is visible offshore.

Located on Mark Island, this lighthouse was established in 1856 to guide ships past dangerous rocks on the sea road to Winter Harbor. The conical brick tower was attached to a keeper's dwelling. A fifth-order lens signaled from the lantern. A larger wood-frame dwelling was built in 1876, and a boathouse was added two years later. When the beacon was converted to kerosene around the turn of the century, an oil house was built.

The lighthouse was decommissioned in 1933 and sold to a private family. The lens was removed, and the duties of the light went to a nearby buoy. The lighthouse remains in private hands and is well maintained. It is not open to the public, but there are distant views from Schoodic Peninsula in Acadia National Park. Some cruises from Bar Harbor and Winter Harbor also provide views.

Ladies in hoop skirts may have had trouble negotiating the tight spiral stairs inside Winter Harbor Lighthouse. Today the station is privately owned, and a buoy does the work the lighthouse once did. *Photograph from the Coast Guard Archives*

# Wood Island Lighthouse
## BIDDEFORD

The light was established on a 35-acre island in 1808 to mark the entrance to the Saco River. The 45-foot octagonal wooden tower initially had a spider lamp, which was replaced circa 1825 by a revolving Lewis light. The lighthouse was rebuilt with granite in 1939, and then rebuilt again in 1858. The 47-foot stone tower was equipped with a fourth-order lens and a fogbell. A spacious dwelling was remodeled in 1906.

**FOR MORE INFORMATION**
Friends of Wood Island
Lighthouse
P.O. Box 26
Biddeford Pool, ME 04006
www.woodislandlighthouse.org

During the 1960s, the Coast Guard removed the lantern from the tower and installed an exposed aerobeacon, which was automated in 1986. A fabricated lantern was returned to the tower during the 1990s. The property is in the care of Friends of Wood Island Lighthouse, a chapter of the American Lighthouse Foundation, which runs frequent tours. Contact them for tour times. The lighthouse is best seen by boat.

The quintessential Maine light station was a sprawl of buildings and walkways. Wood Island Lighthouse was typical, with its quarters attached to the tower by an enclosed walkway and workroom. A pyramidal fogbell tower and oil house completed the station. *Photograph from the author's collection*

# Fogbells, Foghorns, and Fog Dogs

*Hope the fog goes away pretty soon so we'll know there
are other people on this good earth besides ourselves.*
Lightkeeper's Wife
Baker Island, Maine 1953

Much of the work at New England lighthouses was devoted to fog signaling. Lights worked well in clear weather and pierced the murk to some degree, but sound carried through the fog better. A number of devices were used over the years, some of them effective and others a little hair-brained.

The earliest known fog signal was the cannon set up at Boston Light in 1719 and fired every half hour when needed. Plymouth Lighthouse also had cannon. Firing these large guns was hard, dangerous work. Nearly a century passed before a better method was found.

Fogbells came into use in the early nineteenth century. From 1806–1848 Bridgeport, Connecticut, had a bell boat that was tied up in the harbor to work in conjunction with Fayerweather Light. There was no crew. A mast rising from the boat's hull was fitted with five cow bells sounded by wave motion.

West Quoddy Head Light in Maine is credited with having the first lighthouse fogbell, installed in 1820. The keeper sounded it manually with a hammer and was paid an extra $15 per year for the duty. He ended up with plenty of work. The Bay of Fundy, according to historian Jeremy D'Entremont, is rumored to "manufacture fog." Local Indians have a more charming explanation: A mythical giant sometimes smokes his pipe.

Bells soon tolled melodiously from many lighthouses in New England, but not always with success. A famous scientist living within earshot of the fogbell at Rhode Island's Castle Hill Lighthouse had enough political clout to have it removed, citing its noise as intrusive on his studies. Residents of Stratford Point, Connecticut, were more tolerant. Their lighthouse keeper once rang the fogbell by hand for 103 hours, took a short rest, and then resumed tolling the bell for another 103 hours.

Experiments with wave-motion signals were fairly common. Besides the Bridgeport bell boat, there was a

Fog signaling became highly mechanized during the second half of the nineteenth century. Fog trumpets, such as the one in service at Boston Light, were huge and sent loud blares over the water. *Photograph from the Coast Guard Archives*

tidal fogbell at Maine's Whitehead Light. The clapper was connected to a T-bar that was jostled by the waves. It relied, not on the tide, but choppy seas. When the ocean was calm, it was quiet. As is often the case, a foggy day is a calm-water day, so the contraption was not a success.

Maine had several famous fog dogs. Sailor rang the fogbell at Wood Island Lighthouse, while Nemo and Rover did fogbell duty at Heron Neck. Spot, a friendly Springer spaniel that lived at Owls Head Lighthouse in the 1930s gained fame by saving a mail boat in a blizzard. The bell was up to its clapper in snow when Spot heard the distant whistle of the mail boat in distress. He begged to be let out into the storm and bounded to the bell. Digging in the snow, he tried to find the clapper. When this proved useless, he ran down to the water's edge and began barking. The mail boat skipper heard the warning and, not a moment too soon, steered away from the rocks.

Bell strikers came into use about the middle of the nineteenth century and freed keepers and their dogs from the arduous task of manually tolling bells. Whistles, sirens, and horns came along after the Civil War in hopes they might better penetrate the fog. These were useful noisemakers for mariners but not always popular with shore residents. The foghorn at Pomham Rocks Light in 1900 was described in a local newspaper as "the greatest nuisance in the history of the state" with a sound "to make the flesh creep, indescribably lonesome and cheerless. . . and dreary."

As fog signals advanced, specialized buildings were designed to house the complex machinery needed to sound horns, whistles, and sirens. *Photograph from the Coast Guard Archives*

Fog's density can affect the way sound travels, and certain tones work better than others. It was for this reason that the U.S. Lighthouse Board devoted much time and money to fog signal experiments, most of them done at Beavertail Lighthouse at the entrance to the notoriously murky Narragansett Bay. One apparatus was a huge wooden trumpet designed by Celadon Daboll of New London, Connecticut. Daboll came up with various means for sounding the trumpet. The most ingenious method involved a horse walking around a windlass to supply air for the bellows.

In the 1880s, coal-fired boilers raised the steam for whistles, horns, and sirens. Supply ships delivered coal in sacks that were either carried ashore on the back, on horses, or moved from the dock to a storage area on a tram. Keepers coddled the boilers delicate settings and shoveled coal by the ton. Ear-splitting honks, roars, and screeches made big harbors sound like a zoo of wild animals on foggy days. "How about that horrible shrieking and groaning siren that has been stuck up on top of the lighthouse here?" asked a bereft Connecticut senator in 1904 after hearing the new fog signal at New London Light. "This will be the best field of practice for a specialist of nervous disease that I know of," he added

In the early twentieth century, diesel and gasoline engines eased the work of producing steam for fog signals. But electricity was a better solution. It freed the keeper from drudgery and assured a fog signal would sound cheaply, quickly, and regularly. The ultimate advance came after the 1960s when automatic fog sensors and solar batteries, requiring almost no care, replaced keepers. Though unattractive and not nearly as nostalgic and musical as the old bells and horns, these new fog signals get the job done.

Steam-powered fog signals were labor-intensive. Keepers were photographed working in the fog signal building at Block Island's Southeast Lighthouse during the 1930s. *Photograph from the Coast Guard Archives*

Chapter 2

# The Lighthouses of New Hampshire

A commingling of old and new is seen at White Island Lighthouse in the Isles of Shoals. The brick tower and weathered clapboard house with patched roof evoke times past, when families occupied the station. Solar panels, electric foghorns, and modern weather equipment tell of the station's evolution from manual to modern. *Photograph by Shirin Pagels*

# Isles of Shoals Lighthouse
## RYE

A collection of many islets that lie nine miles off Portsmouth, the Isles of Shoals were named for their resemblance to a shoal of fish. An 82-foot stone lighthouse was built on White Island in 1821 to guide ships along the coast and also around the perilous archipelago and into the Piscataqua River. A second lighthouse on the island, constructed in 1859 of granite and brick, stood 58 feet tall and exhibited a second-order Fresnel lens. It was connected to a keeper's quarters by a steep, covered walkway. A fog-bell stood next to the tower.

**FOR MORE INFORMATION**
The Lighthouse Kids
www.thelighthousekids.com

The beacon was automated in 1987 with an acrylic optic and was later solarized. In 1993, the site was deeded to the state of New Hampshire. A group of students from North Hampton, New Hampshire, have been raising money to care for the old lighthouse. The tower was restored in 2005. The station can be seen distantly from shore and is accessible only by boat.

A harmonic view of White Island Light circa 1900 probably was staged for a visiting photographer. The keeper stands on the lantern gallery while his dog plays at the water's edge and a skiff sits on the waves with its sail unfurled, ready for service. *Photograph from the Coast Guard Archives*

# Portsmouth Harbor Lighthouse
## NEW CASTLE

**FOR MORE INFORMATION**
Friends of Portsmouth Harbor
Lighthouse
P.O. Box 8232
Portsmouth, NH 03802
www.portsmouthharbor
lighthouse.org
FPHL@lighthouse.cc

The first beacon for the harbor at Portsmouth was a wooden tower built in 1771 at present-day Fort Constitution. An 80-foot octagonal wooden tower was erected in 1784. It was ceded to the federal government in 1791.

In 1804, the deteriorating lighthouse was razed and a second wooden tower was built. It was illuminated with whale-oil lamps and parabolic reflectors. A new keeper's house was built in 1872. Six years later, the aging lighthouse was replaced by the present-day truncated cast-iron sentinel.

The 48-foot tower held a fourth-order Fresnel lens. It was electrified in 1926 and automated in 1960. An acrylic cylinder now protects the lens and gives it a fixed green characteristic. The site was licensed to the American Lighthouse Foundation in 2000. It is administered by a chapter of the foundation, which holds occasional open houses.

Flanked by the ramparts of Fort Constitution, Portsmouth Harbor Lighthouse casts its green beacon over twilight waters to welcome ships to New Hampshire's largest port. *Photograph by Shirin Pagels*

# GHOSTS ON DUTY

*Asleep or awake, the beacon haunts you.*
George A. Toothaker, Keeper
Halfway Rock Lighthouse 1872–1885

Every lighthouse ought to have a ghost. What better place for a restless spirit to reside than in a damp, tall tower by the sea where storms assail the walls, waves moan and winds squeal, seabirds cry, and eerie veils of fog settle over shipwreck bones?

Lighthouses, by virtue of their location and work, spur the imagination. They are naturally haunted by shadows, sounds, and smells. Their histories are replete with tragic events. Keepers, with time on their hands in the dark of night, imagined all manner of ghosts and goblins and things going bump in the night.

New England has plenty of lighthouse ghost tales, so many that entire books are available about them. Seguin Lighthouse has its ghostly piano music from the phantom fingers of a murdered keeper's wife. New London Ledge Light has a prankster poltergeist named Ernie who steals things, disturbs slumber, and treads softly on the stairs. Owls Head Light has a mysterious invisible keeper who polishes the lens.

At Ram Island Light, a ghost warned vessels off the rocks before the lighthouse was built, then after its commissioning kept the keepers and their families on edge. The same was true of the second lighthouse at Minots Ledge. The keepers of the original tower, who drowned in an 1851 storm, came back to reside in the 1860 masonry tower. One of their favorite unnerving activities was tapping. The source of the metallic sounds was not identified until a logbook revealed that the lost keepers had rapped on a stovepipe to signal each other.

Five Mile Point Light in New Haven, Connecticut, has no known resident haunts, but it creates an ominous silhouette on a full moon night.
*Photograph by Elinor De Wire*

Lighthouse ghost tales are fun and add lots of color to the lore of the sentinels, but most of the stories are old and easily debunked with logical explanations. Lighthouse ghosts have had a tough time keeping up appearances since lighthouses were automated and de-staffed. Many seem to have flown lighthouse purgatory, leaving only spiders and seabirds to haunt the towers.

Maine's Prospect Harbor Light is an exception. The dwelling has been converted to a vacation rental available to military families. The house is comfortably furnished, and nautical decorations adorn the walls, mantle, and windowsills. On one windowsill sit wooden figures of two sailors and a sea captain, looking out to sea. Renters say the center figure of the captain has a life of its own. If facing one direction, it somehow turns itself in another direction without anyone as a witness. Of course, a ghost is the popular explanation, one with quiet feet and mischievous hands.

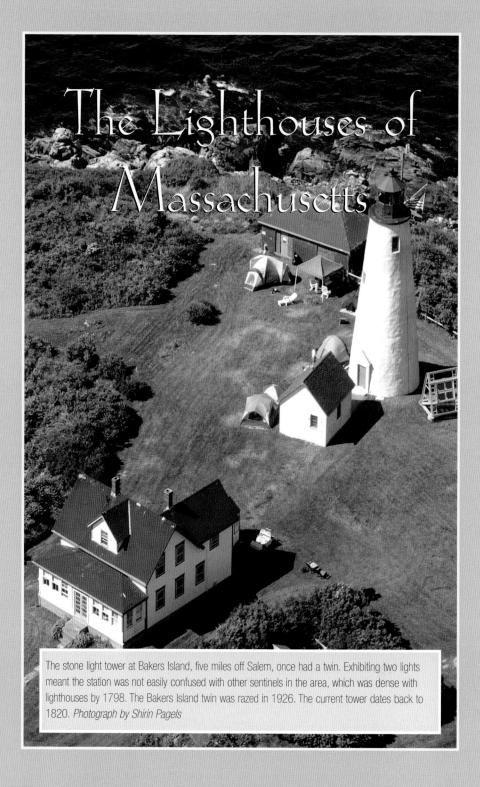

# The Lighthouses of Massachusetts

The stone light tower at Bakers Island, five miles off Salem, once had a twin. Exhibiting two lights meant the station was not easily confused with other sentinels in the area, which was dense with lighthouses by 1798. The Bakers Island twin was razed in 1926. The current tower dates back to 1820. *Photograph by Shirin Pagels*

# Annisquam Lighthouse
## GLOUCESTER

Situated on an old Native American settlement at Wigwam Point, this lighthouse was established in 1801. It was a 32-foot wooden tower with a small wood-frame keeper's dwelling nearby. The beacon probably began as a spider or pan lamp and was later upgraded to a Lewis light. In its early years, it was called Squam Light after the perilous Squam Bar that it marked at the mouth of the Annisquam River.

By 1851, the lighthouse was near collapse. It was an important aid for the local fishing industry, so a new 40-foot octagonal wooden tower was constructed in its place. In 1856, a fifth-order Fresnel lens was installed. A covered walkway connected the tower to the keeper's residence.

**DIRECTIONS**
From MA 127 in Gloucester, take Leonard Street to Elizabeth Road, where there's a sign for Norwood Heights. Turn right on Elizabeth Road, then turn left on Wigwam Road and follow the road to its end. Park in the small lot by the lighthouse. The grounds are private, but the lighthouse can be seen from the parking area.

In 1897, a 41-foot brick tower was built. The lens was fueled by kerosene. In 1922, a fourth-order lens was installed, and the entire station was electrified. A foghorn was added in 1931. The lighthouse operated only from October through June, when fog was most prevalent.

The lighthouse was automated with a modern optic in 1974, and control of the fog signal was moved to a local police station, to be operated as needed. During the 1990s, the station was renovated. Improvements included modernizing the 1801 keeper's house, which was occupied by a Coast Guard family. The lighthouse is not open to visitors. It can be seen from a nearby parking area.

Guarding the Annisquam River at Cape Ann, Annisquam Lighthouse is a Federal-style brick tower. A collectors' card from about 1910 shows radio towers on the site. *Photograph from the author's collection*

# Baker's Island Lighthouse
## SALEM

**DIRECTIONS**

See directions to Marblehead Lighthouse.

Part of a group of islands called the Miseries, 55-acre Baker's Island has been the scene of many shipwrecks. A red daybeacon was erected on the island in 1791, but it was inadequate. In 1798, the first lighthouses were built—twin wooden towers jutting from the roof of a dwelling. These soon deteriorated and were replaced by granite towers in 1820. One tower was taller than the other, so mariners nicknamed them "Mister" and "Missus." The beacons were Lewis lights.

In 1855, the towers were repaired. Four years later, a fourth-order Fresnel lens was installed in the taller tower. A fogbell also was in service by this time. In 1879, a tornado destroyed the fogbell tower. It was repaired a short time later and then entirely replaced in 1907 by a siren. An air horn followed in 1959.

In 1926, the shorter light tower was decommissioned and torn down, ending the twin-light tradition at Baker's Island. The station was electrified in 1938, and automated in 1972. The Fresnel lens was moved to the Shore Village Museum (now the Maine Lighthouse Museum). The 59-foot-tall Mister tower still operates with a solarized modern beacon. The oil house, the foghouse, and two keeper's homes, both built in 1878, also remain.

In 2007, the station was in the process of being transferred to the Essex National Heritage Commission. It is privately owned and is not open to the public. The light can be seen by boat or distantly from land at Chandler Hovey Park.

The stone light tower at Baker's Island, five miles off Salem, once had a twin. Exhibiting two lights meant the station was not easily confused with other sentinels in the area, which was dense with lighthouses by 1798. The Baker's Island twin was razed in 1926. The current tower dates back to 1820. *Photograph from the Coast Guard Archives*

# Bass River Lighthouse
## West Dennis

A private light, shined from a local resident's attic window, was the first navigational aid at the entrance to the Bass River. Shipmasters donated money to keep it lit. In 1855, a lighthouse exhibiting a fourth-order Fresnel lens was built on the beach. It consisted of a lantern constructed on the roof of a two-story dwelling.

In 1880, with the lighting of nearby Stage Harbor Light in Chatham, Bass River Light was decommissioned. It was sold, but just a year later the government bought it back and relit it. The station remained in service until lights placed along the Cape Cod Canal made it obsolete. Bass River Lighthouse was abandoned in 1914 and later sold.

For many years, the lighthouse served as a summer home. It later became an inn and remains so today. The lighthouse was relit with a private beacon in 1989. Guests can arrange to tour the lantern.

**FOR MORE INFORMATION**
The Lighthouse Inn
P.O. Box 128
West Dennis, MA 02670
508.398.2244
www.lighthouseinn.com

**DIRECTIONS**
Travel east on MA 28 in West Dennis, turn right on School Street, turn left on Main Street, and then turn right on Lighthouse Road. The inn is located at the terminus of Lighthouse Road.

High chimneys on Bass River Lighthouse in West Dennis upstaged its small rooftop tower. It's probable the chimneys were raised in height after the station went into service and keepers discovered soot collected on the exterior lantern windows. *Photograph from the Coast Guard Archives*

# Bird Island Lighthouse
## MARION

**FOR MORE INFORMATION**
Bird Island Light Preservation
Society
2 Spring Street
Marion, MA 02738
508.748.0550

Established in 1819 to guide coastal lumber and fishing vessels, this 25-foot stone tower sits on a two-acre islet in Sippican Harbor. A hand-hewn stone stairway gave the tower strength. The revolving beacon, one of the earliest in the region, had ten lamps. It served until 1856, at which time a fourth-order Fresnel lens replaced it. A short time later, a new lantern was installed on the old tower. A fogbell also was added.

An 1869 storm damaged the station, but it continued in service. In 1889, the keeper's dwelling was rebuilt and repairs were made to the lighthouse, including adding six feet to its height. The lighthouse operated until 1933, when lights placed along the Cape Cod Canal made it unnecessary. Five years later, the infamous 1938 hurricane swept away everything at the station except the tower.

The property was sold to private owners in 1940 and then sold to the town of Marion in 1966. A nonprofit group formed to care for the lighthouse, raising funds to have it repaired. The town relit the tower in 1997.

The lighthouse is not open to the public and is accessible only by boat. It is a private aid to navigation maintained by the Bird Island Light Preservation Society. The island is a nesting site for roseate terns.

Bird Island Lighthouse adds beauty to modern-day Sippican Harbor, but its sordid past cannot be erased. One of its early lightkeepers was accused of abusing his wife, abetting her tobacco addiction, and then murdering her. *Photograph by Jeremy D'Entremont*

# Borden Flats Lighthouse
## FALL RIVER

During the 1860s, an unlighted daybeacon was set up on the rubble of rocks and sand at the mouth of the Taunton River. Called Borden Flats, the shallows were a serious hazard to ships that plied the busy textile town of Fall River. In 1881, the daybeacon was removed, and a five-story cast-iron caisson lighthouse was built at a cost of $25,000. It was 48 feet tall and exhibited a fourth-order Fresnel lens fueled by kerosene. A fogbell hung from the lantern deck.

**DIRECTIONS**
From I-195, take RI 138 into Fall River. RI 138 then becomes Broadway. Follow signs toward Tiverton. Turn left on Columbia and then left again on Ponta Delgada. A final left turn onto Ferry Street will take you to the marina.

Summer storms and winter ice floes pummeled the lighthouse, but the worst punishment came in 1938. A great hurricane arrived in September that year, damaging the foundation, but the tower stood firm. After the hurricane, a protective outer caisson was built around the original base.

The lighthouse was not electrified until 1957. Five years later, it was automated. A modern optic was installed in 1977, and the fogbell was replaced by a horn in 1983. The lighthouse is not open to the public. It can be seen from several places along Fall River. The best view is from Borden Light Marina.

The caisson Borden Flats Light was a busy place in the summer of 1900. A boat with two men was photographed landing at its base while the keeper, Martin Thompson, worked in the lantern. *Photograph from the Coast Guard Archives*

# Boston Lighthouse
## LITTLE BREWSTER ISLAND

**FOR MORE INFORMATION**
Friends of Boston
Harbor Islands
P.O. Box 690187
Quincy, MA 02269
781.740.4290
www.fbhi.org

**DIRECTIONS**
To see the lighthouse from shore, take MA 3 south from Boston, through Hingham, and onto Summer Street (at a rotary). Turn left on Washington Boulevard and then merge left onto Nantasket Avenue and drive into Hull. Follow signs for Fort Revere and Telegraph Hill. The lighthouse can be seen from the observation deck on Telegraph Hill.

This lighthouse site is the oldest in the nation. The first sentinel was erected here in 1716 by the Massachusetts Bay Colony. The stone tower was about 50 feet tall and stood on Little Brewster Island. It possibly was illuminated by a chandelier of tallow candles. A keeper's house stood near the tower. In 1719, a fog cannon was set up to signal to ships.

The station suffered several mishaps during its early years, including the drowning of its first two keepers. The third keeper requested a lantern gallery be installed to lessen the dangers of cleaning dirt and snow off the windows. The tower was occasionally struck by lightning, but a worse fate overcame the lighthouse during the American Revolution. It passed back and forth between American and British control and was ultimately blown up by the British in June 1776.

A new stone lighthouse was built in 1783. The 75-foot tower was illuminated with oil lamps. In 1789, it was transferred to the new federal government of the United States. A fogbell was added sometime in 1851. The station was improved in 1859 with the addition of 14 feet of height, a strong brick lining, and a second-order Fresnel lens. A new duplex for keepers also was built.

In 1872, a fog trumpet replaced the old fogbell. During the 1880s, it was changed to a siren. Also at this time, a cistern was built for fresh water, and a second house was added, since there were now three keepers assigned to the station. By the twentieth century, it was a popular family station that often interested reporters and Hollywood film producers.

America's oldest lighthouse site, Boston Light began under British rule at the behest of the Boston Bay Colony in 1716 (**Opposite page** *Photograph from the Coast Guard Academy Library*). It was destroyed during the Revolutionary War but was rebuilt in 1783. Today the site is a national landmark. (**Above** *Photograph by Elinor De Wire*)

During World War II, the light was extinguished to prevent its aiding enemy ships. It went back into service in 1945 and in 1948 was electrified by means of a submarine cable. The keeper's duplex was torn down in 1960 when the Coast Guard decided to use just the smaller keeper's house. A series of keepers lived at the station until 1989, at which time it was announced that the light would be automated and personnel would be removed.

The federal government, fearing vandalism and deterioration at the historic station, offered funding to keep a Coast Guard presence on the island. Several government agencies and nonprofit groups worked to restore and maintain the station and to interpret its history. In 2003, the Coast Guard left the island, and civilian "watchstanders" began taking turns staffing the site.

The lighthouse can be seen from shore in Hull, Winthrop, or Revere. Boat tours are offered by the Boston Harbor Islands Partnership (www.bostonislands.org) and by the Friends of Boston Harbor Islands. Permission to land with a private boat must be obtained by calling the caretaker of the site at 617.223.8666.

# Brandt Point Lighthouse
## NANTUCKET

The second lighthouse to be built in the colonies was at the bustling whaling port on Nantucket Island. Since 1746, the Brant Point Lighthouse has been moved or rebuilt eight times.

In 1856, a 47-foot brick lighthouse was built, connected to a brick keeper's dwelling. A fourth-order Fresnel lens was installed. It served well and worked with several sets of range lights to help mariners safely enter the harbor. In 1900, the brick lighthouse was decommissioned, due to changes on the channel.

The last lighthouse to be erected at Brant Point went into service in 1901. The 26-foot wooden tower exhibited a kerosene-fueled sixth-order Fresnel lens with a red beacon. It also had a fogbell. An oil house was built in 1904. The station was automated in 1965 and was refurbished by the Coast Guard in 2000. Its Fresnel lens continues in operation. The 1856 brick sentinel still stands nearby and is used as part of a Coast Guard station.

Brant Point Light is not open for tours, but the grounds are public. It can be reached on foot a short distance from the ferry slip.

The small wooden lighthouse at Brant Point is a popular tourist attraction in Nantucket Harbor. *Photograph by Shirin Pagels*

# Butler Flats Lighthouse
## New Bedford

Built in 1898, the 53-foot caisson lighthouse replaced the defunct Clark's Point Light. The four-story brick tower and iron foundation were constructed on mudflats in the channel that led into busy New Bedford Harbor. The tower exhibited a fifth-order Fresnel lens fueled by kerosene and had a fogbell. It was painted red, then changed to white a year later. Stone riprap was placed around the base of the lighthouse to protect it from ice.

After the 1938 hurricane, which did little damage to the lighthouse but which flooded the city, a hurricane barrier was built across the entrance to New Bedford Harbor. Lights on the barrier reduced the need for Butler Flats Light. In 1978, the Coast Guard gave the sentinel to the city of New Bedford, at which time it also was solarized. After the beacon was vandalized in 1998, a new optic was installed with a submarine power cable from shore.

Volunteers care for the light, but it is not open to the public. It can be seen from East Rodney French Boulevard in New Bedford. For a closer view, ride the ferry that runs from New Bedford to Martha's Vineyard, or from New Bedford to Cuttyhunk.

The cylindrical tiers of Butler Flats Lighthouse evoke a castle parapet. It guards a sandbar in the harbor at New Bedford. *Photograph by Shirin Pagels*

# Cape Poge Lighthouse
## CHAPPAQUIDDICK ISLAND

**FOR MORE INFORMATION**
Cape Poge Wildlife
Refuge Dike Road,
Chappaquiddick Island,
Martha's Vineyard, MA 02539
508.627.7689
www.thetrustees.org/capepoge
wildliferefuge.cfm
islands@ttot.org

The lighthouse was established in 1801 on the northeast tip of Martha's Vineyard to guide ships into Edgartown. The 35-foot octagonal wooden tower exhibited oil lamps. Erosion ate away the shore by the tower, eventually claiming the keeper's dwelling. In 1838, the tower had to be dismantled and moved farther away from the sea. Soon, the entire station rotted and was considered inadequate.

A new lighthouse was built in 1844 at a cost of $1,600. In 1857, a fourth-order Fresnel lens replaced the old lamps and reflectors. Erosion continued to be a problem. In 1878, the keeper's dwelling was rebuilt on a safer site farther away from the sea. Two years later, the lighthouse also was rebuilt in a safer location. These measures proved temporary, and in 1893 a fifth light tower was built.

The 40-foot wooden tower was moved four times during the 1900s. It was automated in 1943, and the dwelling was sold and torn down. In 1987, the final move was accomplished by helicopter. The tower was renovated, and a modern automatic optic was installed.

The lighthouse sits on a wildlife refuge. It is accessible only via a four-wheel-drive vehicle. Permits are available from the trustees of the refuge, who also offer occasional summer tours of the lighthouse.

Chappaquiddick Island owes its fame to the Kennedy family, but long before their summer home was built on the island, Cape Poge Lighthouse stood watch on the northeast tip. The station was established in 1801. The current wooden tower was constructed in 1893.
*Photograph by Shirin Pagels*

# Chatham Lighthouse
## CHATHAM

Twin wooden light towers, each 40 feet tall and situated 70 feet apart, were built in 1808 to help ships negotiate the treacherous elbow of Cape Cod into Nantucket Sound. The lanterns each had a Lewis light of six lamps and reflectors. After erosion threatened the wooden towers, they were replaced in 1841 by twin 40-foot brick towers.

In 1857, the twins were improved with fourth-order fixed Fresnel lenses. Erosion continued its assault, and by 1877 the towers were less than 50 feet from the sea. Two new lighthouses were built. The handsome cast-iron edifices flanked a large Victorian dwelling. The Fresnel lenses from the defunct towers were transferred to the new towers, and the fuel was changed from lard oil to kerosene in 1888. The towers continued in operation until 1923, at which time the north tower was loaded onto a barge and moved up the cape to Nauset Beach, where it remains on duty today.

The remaining south tower was converted to an incandescent oil vapor light in 1923 and then electrified in 1939. In 1969, the old lantern was replaced by a new one, and a modern optic was installed. The old lantern and lens were moved to the Atwood House Museum in Chatham. After automation in 1982, the Coast Guard continued to occupy the quarters. The lighthouse is not open to the public, except on special occasions. The grounds are open year-round, and there is parking near the site.

**FOR MORE INFORMATION**
Nobska Coast Guard Auxiliary
508.430.0628

**DIRECTIONS**
Driving east on MA 28, bear right at the Chatham rotary onto Main Street. Follow Main Street through Chatham to a sharp right where Main Street intersects with Shore Road. Continue south on Main Street about a half mile to the lighthouse parking area.

Chatham Light, Chatham, Mass.

Chatham Lighthouse was a busy station during World War II. Like many sentinels, it did double duty as a navigational aid and a coastal watch station. A lookout tower and beach patrol were headquartered here. Weather flags were posted on the flagpole in front of the lighthouse, and an air-raid siren stood on a tall post behind the tower. *Photograph from the author's collection*

# Clark's Point Lighthouse
## NEW BEDFORD

**DIRECTIONS**

Follow directions to the Palmer Island Lighthouse viewing area. Leave Twin Pier and turn right on Potomska Street, then turn left on Front Street. Turn left on Cove Road and then turn right on East Rodney French Boulevard. Follow the signs to Fort Taber.

As early as 1797, merchants in New Bedford placed a simple wooden lighthouse at the entrance to the harbor to assist vessels arriving from Buzzards Bay. This first lighthouse burned down in 1798 and was rebuilt in 1799. The second lighthouse burned down in August 1803. It was replaced in 1804 by a 42-foot stone lighthouse. A small saltbox dwelling sat near the tower.

The lantern, lamps, and reflectors were improved in 1851, but it is not known if a Fresnel lens was installed. In 1860, the lighthouse lost importance when nearby Fort Taber was built. The fort's walls obscured the light, necessitating the relocation of the lantern and the beacon to the fort wall. The light served until 1898, at which time Butler Flats Light went into service. The old stone Clark's Point tower was demolished in 1906.

The obsolete light on the fort enjoyed a redux when the City of New Bedford restored and relit it in June 2001. Although the lighthouse is not yet open to the public, it can be visited as part of the public park at Fort Taber.

Mariners and citizens of New Bedford lamented the loss of the beacon in Clark's Point Light after it was decommissioned in 1898. The lighthouse stood dark for more than a century. In 2001, after this photograph was taken, the city ceremoniously returned the light to the tower. *Photograph from the New Bedford Department of Tourism & Marketing*

# Cleveland East Ledge Lighthouse
## BOURNE

C ompleted in 1943 to mark the western entrance into Cape Cod Canal, this lighthouse was the last lighthouse built in New England. The ledge took its name from President Grover Cleveland, who enjoyed fishing in the area. The 70-foot steel and reinforced-concrete tower and caisson began service with a kerosene-fueled fourth-order Fresnel lens. Coast Guard keepers lived in the modern quarters below the tower.

Other than minor damage during a 1944 hurricane, the lighthouse had an uneventful career. It was automated in 1978 with a modern flashing white optic that was powered by an electric submarine cable. A foghorn is mounted on the deck. The lighthouse was refurbished in 1990. It is not accessible to the public and can be seen only by boat.

The moderne-style lighthouse at Cleveland Ledge is one of New England's youngest sentinels, built in 1943 by the Coast Guard. It guides vessels into the Cape Cod Canal and is named for President Grover Cleveland, who enjoyed fishing in its surrounding waters during the 1880s and 1890s. *Photograph by Frederick A. Medina*

# Deer Island Lighthouse
## WINTHROP

A stone daybeacon was set up a short distance south of the island in 1832 and was the only navigational aid until 1890, at which time a 51-foot caisson lighthouse was built about a quarter-mile from the island to mark the Presidents Roads Channel. The lantern exhibited a fixed white light, and the exterior was painted brown.

The lighthouse endured the great Portland Gale of 1898, when seawater washed over its lantern. The Portland Gale was named for the passenger steamer *Portland*, which passed close to the lighthouse before it sank with almost 200 people aboard.

A severe storm in February 1972 spelled the end of the lighthouse. After this storm, the lighthouse crew was removed and no repairs were made. The lighthouse continued to deteriorate. In 1982, it was razed and replaced by a modern fiberglass tower. The new lighthouse, looking much like a lighted cigarette jutting out of the water, cost $100,000 and was designed to withstand powerful winds.

Complaints about the ultra-modern light resulted in a new structure. In 1983, a 33-foot brown fiberglass light was erected at the site of the old caisson. It continues to serve shipping vessels. It is not accessible to the public but can be seen from the walking trail around the perimeter of Deer Island.

Boston Harbor has several lighthouses, including Deer Island Light. It began its career as a cast-iron caisson sentinel a few hundred feet off the island. During the 1980s, it was replaced by a fiberglass tower. The island is now occupied by a sewage treatment plant. *Photograph from the author's collection*

# Derby Wharf Lighthouse
## SALEM

This tiny lighthouse was built in 1871 to guide vessels into Salem Harbor. It altered the role of the twin lighthouses at Baker's Island. The 23-foot brick tower—supposedly the shortest in the nation—exhibited a red, fixed, fifth-order beacon. A caretaker was hired to maintain it, eliminating the need for a keeper's dwelling.

In 1906, it was upgraded to a fourth-order light and then downgraded in 1910 to a sixth-order lens when shipping traffic decreased in Salem. The beacon was electrified during the early 1970s. It was deactivated in 1977, and ownership was transferred to the National Park Service in 1979. Four years later, a nonprofit group relit the beacon with a solar optic. It was refurbished in 1989 and today operates as a private aid to navigation. The lighthouse is not open to the public but can be viewed from the Salem Maritime National Historic Site.

**FOR MORE INFORMATION**
Salem Maritime National
Historic Site
174 Derby Street
Salem, MA 01970
www.nps.gov/sama

**DIRECTIONS**
From MA 114 in Salem, turn right on Derby Street and drive to the historic waterfront. The lighthouse sits on the rock pier jutting into the harbor.

On a gray winter day, a blanket of snow surrounds the 1871 Derby Wharf Lighthouse. The Salem sentinel is the shortest lighthouse in the United States.
*Photograph by Shirin Pagels*

# Duxbury Pier Lighthouse
## PLYMOUTH

**FOR MORE INFORMATION**
Project Gurnet and Bug Lights
P.O. Box 2167
Duxbury, MA 02331
www.buglight.org

This 47-foot caisson lighthouse was built in 1871 to mark a dangerous shoal on the north side of the entrance to Plymouth Harbor. Mariners affectionately called it Bug Light. The lantern displayed a fourth-order Fresnel lens and had a fogbell mounted on the outside. A few years after it was established, a gallery was built around it to protect the keepers as they worked and to facilitate access. Stone riprap also was placed around the tower to ward off ice. The lighthouse survived the horrendous 1944 hurricane with minor damage.

The sentinel was automated in 1964, and a modern optic replaced the classical lens. Vandalism and the elements took a toll on the tower. In 1983, the Coast Guard announced plans to raze the structure. A nonprofit group raised funds to repair the lighthouse, giving it a temporary reprieve, but vandalism again became a problem. A thorough restoration of Duxbury Pier Lighthouse was completed in 2001. The lighthouse is not open to the public and is best seen by boat.

An antique postcard captured the lightkeeper in his boat at the base of Duxbury Pier Lighthouse. Ropes for raising and lowering the boat hung from the left side of the tower. The artist exaggerated the lantern with yellow window panes. *Photograph from the author's collection*

# East Chop Lighthouse
## MARTHA'S VINEYARD

I n British parlance, *chop* refers to a channel entrance. In colonial days the term was applied to the entrance to Vineyard Haven Harbor. For many years, the eastern side of the channel had a semaphore station that was used to relay information about the arrival of ships. This earned it the name Telegraph Hill.

In 1869, a private light tower was built on the site, but it burned down three years later. The light was then placed atop a house. In 1878, the Lighthouse Board established on the site a government lighthouse that was often called Telegraph Hill Light. A quainter nickname was Chocolate Light, in honor of its brown daymark. In 1988, the tower was painted white.

The 40-foot cast-iron tower stood on Oak Bluffs. It was lined with bricks for stability and sported Italianate ornamentation to dress up its otherwise plain design. The single whale-oil lamp was intensified with a Fresnel lens. A handsome wooden dwelling stood nearby. An oil house was added a few years after the light was converted to kerosene.

The lighthouse was automated in 1933, and the dwelling and the oil house were razed the following year. The light continues in operation, sending a green flash over the harbor. In 1994, it was leased to the Martha's Vineyard Historical Society. The group offers sunset tours from mid-June through mid-September. Contact them for dates and reservations.

Wire mesh surrounds the lantern of East Chop Lighthouse to ward off migrating birds attracted to the light. A closer look at the railing reveals iron finials in the shape of miniature lighthouses. *Photograph by Kraig Anderson*

**FOR MORE INFORMATION**
Martha's Vineyard Historical Society
P.O. Box 1310
Edgartown, MA 02539
508.627.4441
www.marthasvineyardhistory.org

**DIRECTIONS**
From the ferry dock at Martha's Vineyard, turn left on Water Street and then left on Beach Road. Turn left on Temahigan Avenue, which ends at Highland Drive. Turn left and drive to the lighthouse.

# Eastern Point Lighthouse
## GLOUCESTER

**DIRECTIONS**
At the intersection of MA 128 and MA 127A in Gloucester, take East Main Street. It becomes Eastern Point Road and then Eastern Point Boulevard. Enter a private road and drive to a parking area near the lighthouse. (Access is permitted for lighthouse viewers.) The lighthouse is best seen by walking a short distance out onto the breakwater.

A 30-foot stone lighthouse was established in 1832 to mark the entrance to Gloucester Harbor. It had ten whale-oil lamps with reflectors. The lighthouse was not well built and shuddered miserably during storms. In 1847, the need for a better light became paramount, with the opening of a rail line into Gloucester.

A new 34-foot stone lighthouse was built with eleven lamps and reflectors that shone through the lantern's red glass windows. In 1857, the station was improved with a fogbell and a fourth-order Fresnel lens. The bell was lost during an 1869 storm. A few years later, the light was changed from fixed red to flashing red.

In 1890, a third 36-foot brick tower was constructed on the foundation of the original lighthouse. A duplex dwelling that had been built in 1879 was attached to the tower via a covered walkway. An oil house was added in 1894, but it soon became obsolete when an electric cable was laid to the station in 1897.

Also constructed during this period was a stone breakwater extending some 750 yards into the harbor. Dog Bar Light, also called Gloucester Breakwater Light, was built at the end of the breakwater and became the responsibility of the lightkeepers. It marked both the breakwater and a dangerous reef.

The station was automated in 1985. Coast Guard families lived in the quarters for a few years. Today the quarters are empty. The station is not open to the public but can be seen from the breakwater.

An elaborate wooden scaffold held aloft the fogbell at Eastern Point Lighthouse until about 1860. The bell was elevated to accommodate the fall of weights from the clockworks system that powered its automatic striker. A storm in 1869 destroyed the bell tower. *Photograph from the Coast Guard Archives*

# Edgartown Harbor Lighthouse
## MARTHA'S VINEYARD

The bustling whaling town of Martha's Vineyard was marked with a lighthouse in 1828. The sentinel exhibited whale-oil lamps. It was built on a wooden pier in the harbor and consisted of a tower built on the roof of a two-story house. In 1830, it was connected to shore by a wooden walkway. The pier had to be rebuilt of stone in 1839, and in 1847 the walkway was demolished and replaced by a stone breakwater.

Circa 1855, the lighthouse was equipped with a fourth-order Fresnel lens and a fogbell. The lighthouse stood firm until it was irreparably damaged during the 1938 hurricane. It was demolished and replaced with a 45-foot cast-iron tower that had served in Ipswich. The new light was automated.

In 1985, the lighthouse got a facelift when it was sandblasted and repainted. Today it is leased to the Martha's Vineyard Historical Society. A children's memorial was established at the base of the tower in 2001.

**FOR MORE INFORMATION**
See East Chop Lighthouse.

**DIRECTIONS**
From the ferry dock in Vineyard Haven, turn left on Main Street and then turn left on Edgartown Road, which becomes Main Street near Edgartown. Turn left on Water Street and drive to a view of the lighthouse. A walking trail from Water Street leads to the lighthouse.

The original Edgartown Lighthouse was destroyed during the infamous September 1938 hurricane. Its replacement, a 45-foot cast-iron tower, was disassembled at Crane's Beach in Ipswich, moved to Edgartown on a barge, and reassembled as the new Edgartown Light. *Photograph by Shirin Pagels*

# Fort Pickering Lighthouse
## SALEM

**FOR MORE INFORMATION**
Winter Island Marine
Recreational Park
50 Winter Island Road
Salem, MA 01970
978.745-9430
winterisland@cove.com

**DIRECTIONS**
From highway 1A in Salem, drive east on Webb Street. Turn left on Derby Street, and continue to Winter Island and the park. Bear left inside the park to drive to the lighthouse.

Located on Winter Island, this lighthouse was built in 1871 to mark the tricky approach to Salem Harbor. Along with Derby Wharf Light, it served to guide ships in the main channel. The 28-foot iron and brick tower stood in the water and was connected to a two-story wooden dwelling by an elevated walkway.

In 1934, a Coast Guard air base was established on the island. A decade later, the base became a sea and air rescue facility. The lighthouse was decommissioned in 1969, and an offshore buoy took over its functions. After a 1978 storm damaged the tower, a group formed to refurbish it. They relit it in 1983 as a private aid to navigation. The lighthouse is part of a park. It is not open to the public, but visitors may tour the grounds.

Only a white coat of paint prevents Fort Pickering Light from camouflaging itself against the brown rocks of Salem Harbor. Painted daymarks, even plain ones, helped mariners find light towers during the day. *Photograph by Kristin Scroope*

# Gay Head Lighthouse
## MARTHA'S VINEYARD

The colorful cliffs on the southwestern tip of Martha's Vineyard were marked with a 54-foot octagonal wooden sentinel in 1799. The lantern was illuminated with a spider lamp that burned whale oil. The area surrounding the lighthouse belonged to the Wampanoag nation, who often assisted the lightkeeper.

A revolving, ten-lamp Lewis light was installed circa 1812. A new lantern was fitted on the tower in 1837. A few years later, erosion of the cliff forced the inland relocation of the tower. Its duties were soon passed to a new lighthouse.

In 1856, a 51-foot brick tower was erected. Its first-order Fresnel lens, equipped with an eclipser (a panel with open slots turned around the light source) that produced a flash, had been exhibited at the World's Fair in Paris. The price tag for the opulent lens was $16,000, almost half the cost of the tower. In 1902, a new dwelling was built. The fuel was changed to kerosene in 1912. A modern optic was installed in 1952, and the Fresnel lens went on display at the Martha's Vineyard Historical Society Museum.

**FOR MORE INFORMATION**
See East Chop Lighthouse.

**DIRECTIONS**
From the ferry dock at Vineyard Haven, turn left on Main Street, which becomes State Road. Follow the road southwest through Chilmark, then west through Aquinnah, where you can view the lighthouse.

Like many picturesque lighthouses, the sentinel at Gay Head did double duty as a beacon for ships and a tourist attraction. A vintage postcard shows visitors at the station circa 1900. *Photograph from the author's collection*

# Graves Lighthouse
## WINTHROP

The Graves, a rock ledge in outer Boston Harbor, snagged many vessels before a navigational aid marked it. The first aid was a bell buoy sunk off the rocks in 1854. Shipwrecks continued, but the government delayed marking the rocks with a lighthouse, citing more urgent projects.

By 1900, a new channel had been dredged for ships entering Boston. A strong masonry lighthouse was built at a cost of $188,000. Stone was quarried from Cape Ann and shipped to Lovell's Island in Boston Harbor, which became the staging point for construction. The 113-foot Graves Lighthouse was completed in 1905. The majestic granite tower exhibited a first-order Fresnel lens seated on a mercury float, to facilitate rotation. It was the most powerful light in New England at the time.

The lighthouse was automated and unmanned in 1976. Its great lens was removed and sent to the Smithsonian Institution. Vandalism soon took a toll on the tower, and powerful storms during 1991 and 2001 damaged the station and broke the submarine cable supplying power to the light. It was then converted to solar power.

The lighthouse is not open to the public and is off-limits to boaters. It can be seen from Winthrop Beach and from Hull's Nantasket Beach to the south. Lighthouse cruises offered by the Friends of the Boston Harbor Islands and by Boston Harbor Cruises pass by the light.

Though its name suggests a pelagic cemetery lies beneath it, the namesake for Graves Light was actually a colonial merchant named Thomas Graves. The site was a hazard for ships entering Boston Harbor beginning in the early 1600s, but its lighthouse was not completed until 1905. *Photograph by Darlene Cook*

# Great Point Lighthouse
## NANTUCKET

A wooden lighthouse was erected at this site in 1785 to warn vessels passing between Monomoy and Nantucket and to provide guidance into Nantucket Harbor. The keeper rode a horse 14 miles round-trip each day to tend the beacon. A house was added circa 1790 but burned down in 1812. It was replaced, but only four years later, the entire station burned.

A 60-foot stone lighthouse was built in 1818. It was equipped with two tiers of fourteen lamps and reflectors, which served until 1857, at which time a third-order Fresnel lens was installed.

A dwelling for an assistant keeper was built, and the tower, unstable from years of weathering storms, was given a brick lining. Keepers continued to care for the station until the station was automated during the 1950s. The keeper's dwelling burned in 1966.

The lighthouse sits on a wildlife refuge. An over-sand vehicle permit must be purchased to drive to the lighthouse. Daily tours are offered from May through September by the trustees of the site. Contact the refuge for reservations and fees.

**FOR MORE INFORMATION**
Coskata-Coatue Wildlife Refuge
508.228.5646
www.thetrustees.org/pages/
293_coskata_coatue_wildlife_
refuge.cfm
islands@ttor.org

**DIRECTIONS**
From the ferry dock in Nantucket, drive onto Broad Street, turn left on South Water Street, and then turn right on Main Street. Turn left on Orange Street and continue to a rotary. At the rotary, turn east on Milestone Road, then turn left onto Polpis Road, and then turn left onto Wauwinet Road. Continue to the gate for Coskata-Coatue Wildlife Refuge.

Destroyed by a storm on its two-hundredth birthday in 1984, the original Great Point Light rose from the rubble like a phoenix when local citizens had it rebuilt two years later. Upon its completion, Senator Edward Kennedy christened the replica tower with a bottle of champagne. *Photograph by Shirin Pagels*

# Highland Lighthouse
## TRURO

**FOR MORE INFORMATION**
Highland Museum & Lighthouse
P.O. Box 486
Truro, MA 02666
508.487.1121
www.trurohistorical.org

**HOURS OF OPERATION**
The lighthouse is open daily for tours May through October from 10:00 A.M. until 5:30 P.M. The grounds are open year-round.

**DIRECTIONS**
From MA 6 three miles north of Truro, take the Cape Cod Light/Highland Road exit and drive east on Highland Road to South Highland Road. Turn right at South Highland Road and then turn left on Lighthouse Road. Park in the lot west of the lighthouse, which is about a ten-minute walk from the lot.

Also called Cape Cod Light, this sentinel was established in 1797 on a high bluff overlooking Peaked Hill Bars, an area of submerged sandbars. The wooden lighthouse was 45 feet tall and fitted with whale-oil lamps and reflectors.

In 1811, the tower was shortened by 17 feet and a new lantern was installed. A Lewis light replaced the eclipser. In 1831, a new brick lighthouse was built, followed by a new keeper's dwelling in 1856.

In 1857, a third lighthouse was built; it was equipped with a first-order Fresnel lens. A fog signal also was installed at this time as well, and two assistants were hired to help the keeper.

A larger lens was installed in 1902, making the light the most powerful in New England. Electricity was installed in 1932, and a modern optic was added in the 1950s.

The station was automated in 1986. A decade later, erosion forced the relocation of the lighthouse 450 feet to the west.

The station was a popular destination throughout its career. Car travelers during the 1920s let air out of their tires in order to negotiate the soft sandy road to the lighthouse. *Photograph from the author's collection*

# Hospital Point Lighthouse
## BEVERLY

This 1872 lighthouse was built at the site of an early nineteenth-century smallpox hospital. It guided sea traffic into Salem Harbor and Beverly Harbor. The square, 45-foot brick tower exhibited a rare fixed 3.5-order Fresnel lens. It had an unusual condensing panel that made the light dim if a ship entering the channel veered off course. A roomy two-story house stood next to the tower.

In 1927, a light in the steeple of a nearby church began working with the beacon at Hospital Point to provide a rear range light for ships in the channel. Hospital Point Light served as the front range. This arrangement continues today. Hospital Point Light was automated in 1947.

**FOR MORE INFORMATION**
Beverly City Hall
191 Cabot Street
Beverly, MA 01915
978.921.6000
www.beverlyma.gov

**DIRECTIONS**
Drive north on 1A in Beverly and turn right on Dane Street, which becomes Hale Street. Turn right on Corning Street and then turn right on Bayview Avenue. The lighthouse can be seen from the end of the street.

One of the perks for commanders of the First Coast Guard District is a home in the quarters at Hospital Point Lighthouse in Beverly. The Federal-design tower stands guard over the well-appointed house and, according to one commander's wife interviewed by a newspaper reporter, "makes a nice lamp post."
*Photograph by Shirin Pagels*

# Hyannis Lighthouse
## Barnstable

**DIRECTIONS**

The lighthouse can be seen from Orrin Keyes Beach in Hyannis. From Rt.28 in Hyannis, bear left onto W. Main Street, then right on Pitchers Way. Turn left on Marston Avenue and proceed straight onto Hyannis Avenue. Watch for a sign for Orrin Keyes Beach.

A lamp in the window of a privately owned beach shack provided the first aid to mariners entering Hyannis Harbor. In 1849, it was replaced by a small brick tower fitted with oil lamps and reflectors. A red sector warned of Southwest Shoal. The man who had maintained the private light was appointed keeper of the new tower. A keeper's dwelling was added in 1850, attached to the tower by a covered walkway.

In 1856, the lantern was fitted with a new fifth-order Fresnel lens. A new lantern was installed shortly thereafter, to replace the old birdcage-style lantern. In 1885, the lighthouse became the rear range light working in tandem with a small wooden light tower on a nearby wharf. The lighthouse was decommissioned in 1929 and sold to private owners. It is not open to the public and can be seen only by boat.

Prior to the National Historic Preservation Act of 1966, lighthouses that outlived their usefulness were sold to the highest bidder. Hyannis Harbor Light, deactivated in 1929 after seventy years of service, has been in private hands for several generations. *Photograph by Bob Scroope*

# Long Island Head Lighthouse
## BOSTON

The first lighthouse at this site was a 23-foot stone sentinel built in 1819 on a high hill overlooking the harbor. It guided vessels into Boston through Broad Sound Channel. The beacon was provided by nine oil lamps and reflectors. But the lighthouse was poorly constructed and was thus replaced in 1844 with a cast-iron tower, the first of its kind in the nation. A small saltbox-style keeper's dwelling also was built at this time.

In 1881, a third lighthouse was constructed, again of cast iron. When nearby Fort Strong was expanded in 1900, the station was rebuilt at a new location. The 52-foot brick tower, the fourth lighthouse to stand duty on the island, had an attached workroom. It was automated in 1929. The Coast Guard shut down the light for a short time during the 1980s but later relit it using a solar beacon. The island and lighthouse are not open to the public, but the tower can be seen by boat.

Long Island Light, Boston Harbor.

With a commanding view of Boston Harbor, Long Island Head was an excellent site for a lighthouse. Three towers have stood at the site, including the current cast-iron sentinel built in 1881. *Photograph from the author's collection*

# Long Point Lighthouse
## PROVINCETOWN

**FOR MORE INFORMATION**
American Lighthouse
Foundation
P.O. Box 565
Rockland, ME 04841

**DIRECTIONS**
At the terminus of MA 6A in Provincetown, turn left on Province Lands Road and park in Pilgrims First Landing Park. From here, hike across the breakwater and the sand to the lighthouse. The hike passes near Wood End Lighthouse.

The first lighthouse at this site was a wooden cottage-style sentinel that went into service in 1826. It marked the northern tip of Cape Cod. The lantern projected from the roof of the dwelling and exhibited ten lamps and reflectors. A settlement of fishing families lived on the point, along with the lightkeeper.

The station received a new sixth-order Fresnel lens in 1856. By the 1870s, however, the lighthouse was in shambles. A new square brick tower was built in 1875, along with an attached half-story dwelling. A fogbell was installed at this time as well.

The station was automated in 1952 and modernized in 1982, at which time the Fresnel lens was replaced by a solar optic. The lighthouse is not open to the public but is maintained by the Cape Cod chapter of the American Lighthouse Foundation. It can be viewed by boat or reached by a long, strenuous hike across a stone breakwater and a beach.

Built on sands where the Pilgrims walked, Long Point Light was a pleasant, albeit remote, assignment on Cape Cod. A vintage postcard suggests the lightkeeper had leisure time. *Photograph by Jeremy D'Entremont*

# Marblehead Lighthouse
## MARBLEHEAD

Marking the entrance to the harbor, the first lighthouse at this site was a 20-foot brick tower lit in 1835. It was attached to a dwelling by means of a covered walkway. The beacon was fueled by whale oil. By 1880, so many homes had been built around the tiny lighthouse that it could no longer be seen from sea. The light was moved to the top of a 100-foot mast.

In 1896, the post was replaced by a 100-foot cast-iron skeleton lighthouse, painted brown. It was the only sentinel of this design in New England. The tower's sixth-order Fresnel lens served until automation in 1960, at which time the dwelling was torn down. The lighthouse sits in a park but is not open to the public. It is leased to the town of Marblehead and cared for by a local Rotary Club.

**FOR MORE INFORMATION**
Town of Marblehead
www.marblehead.org

**DIRECTIONS**
Drive north on MA 129 in Marblehead and turn right on Ocean Avenue. Cross the causeway, then bear left on Harbor Avenue, which connects to Ocean Avenue again. Make a left on Follett Street and watch for signs for Chandler Hovey Park. The lighthouse sits in the park. Baker's Island Light is visible offshore from the park.

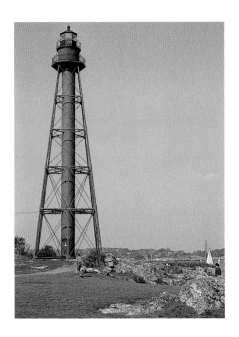

Less beautiful than many of its sister sentries, the skeleton-tower lighthouse at Marblehead Neck replaced a more traditional brick tower in 1896. It watches over thousands of recreational boaters each year, including those who compete in a popular yacht race. *Photograph by Elinor De Wire*

# Minots Ledge Lighthouse
## SCITUATE

The first lighthouse at this site was an iron skeleton tower lighted in 1850 at a cost of $39,000. Its pile legs were anchored to a rocky ledge a mile offshore from the town of Cohasset. The beacon guided ships into Boston, past the dangerous Minots Ledge.

The lighthouse was not sturdy, and it collapsed into the sea during a storm in April 1851, killing two keepers. Its successor was a lightship, anchored on-site until a stone tower was completed in 1860. The 114-foot lighthouse held a second-order Fresnel lens and had a fogbell suspended from its lantern. Homes for the keepers' families were built ashore. In 1894, the optic was changed to a third-order lens, and the beacon began signaling its famous 1-4-3 "I LOVE YOU" flashing light characteristic in order to differentiate it from other lights in the area.

Due to the difficulty of living in the sea-swept tower, it was automated in 1947. It was refurbished in 1989 and given a modern optic. A replica of the lantern containing the Fresnel lens sits ashore on Government Island. Also on display are the fogbell and the renovated keeper's house. The lighthouse is not open and is best seen by boat. It is visible in the distance from various points along Atlantic Avenue, northeast of Cohasset.

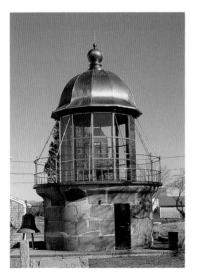

A grand engineering experiment, the second Minots Ledge Lighthouse was modeled after Scotland's famous Bell Rock Light. In 1860, it was firmly anchored in the ledge a mile offshore, and it has withstood countless storms. (*Left: Photograph from the author's collection*) In 1989, the tower was refurbished and updated with a modern optic. Its lantern was brought ashore for restoration, and a replica was made to display the defunct Fresnel lens. The replica with lens (**Above:** *Photograph by Elinor De Wire*) sits on Government Island.

# Monomoy Point Lighthouse
## CHATHAM

This lighthouse was built in 1823 at the tip of an eight-mile-long sand spit that extended south from the elbow of Cape Cod. The wooden tower was incorporated into the roof of a brick keeper's dwelling. It exhibited eight lamps and reflectors to warn mariners of shoals and swift currents off the point. By 1849, the structure was too leaky and unstable to continue service. It was replaced by a cast-iron tower and a new wooden keeper's house. In 1857, it was upgraded with a fourth-order Fresnel lens.

**FOR MORE INFORMATION**
Manager, Monomoy Wildlife Refuge
Wikis Way, Morris Island
Chatham, MA 02633
508.945.0594
www.monomoy.fws.gov

In 1882, the lighthouse was painted with a red daymark. A decade later, it was stabilized with exterior iron supports, giving it the odd appearance of having spindly legs. The light was abandoned in 1923 after shipping was diverted to the Cape Cod Canal.

The lighthouse was sold to a private owner and later became the property of the Massachusetts Audubon Society. It is located on Monomoy Wildlife Refuge. It is not accessible except by special arrangement with the U.S. Fish and Wildlife Service.

The 1849 Monomoy Point Lighthouse no longer serves mariners at night, but it has a colorful red daymark and an equally colorful history. Local Native Americans used the sand spit as a summer encampment for fishing and hunting. Mooncussing, or luring ships onto the shoals with false lights, was practiced here during the 1600s. By the time the lighthouse was established on Monomoy Point in 1823, whaling and merchant ships were numerous. The light was no longer needed after the Cape Cod Canal opened in 1914. *Photograph by Kraig Anderson*

# Nauset Beach Lighthouse and the Three Sisters Lights
## EASTHAM

**FOR MORE INFORMATION**
Nauset Light Preservation Society
P.O. Box 941
Eastham, MA 02642
www.nausetlight.org

**DIRECTIONS**
Drive north on MA 6 at Eastham and turn right onto Nauset Road, which becomes Doane Road. Turn left on Oceanview Avenue and drive to the beach parking area. Nauset Light is a short walk north. The Sisters stand in a wooded area a short walk west on Cable Road.

The first beacons on this site were three 15-foot wooden towers erected in 1838 on the bluffs overlooking Nauset Beach. Nicknamed the Three Sisters, the lights signaled to inshore vessels traveling along the backside of Cape Cod. They were situated 150 feet apart, with a wooden dwelling standing to the north. In 1856, their lamps and reflectors were replaced by three sixth-order Fresnel lenses. Twenty years later, they were upgraded to fourth-order lenses.

Erosion continually consumed the bluff. In 1890, new triple towers were built, and an oil house was added, since the fuel was now kerosene. By 1911, erosion again threatened the lighthouses. One was moved back from the bluff, and the other two were sold to private owners. In 1923, the last Sister was decommissioned and replaced by one of the twin lights from Chatham.

The cast-iron tower was brought from Chatham to Nauset by barge and was fitted with the fourth-order lens from the defunct Sister. It was later painted with a red band. The station was automated in 1955 and the house was sold. In 1975, the Sisters were purchased from their private owners and placed on display in a wooded area of Eastham. Nauset Beach Light was moved back from the bluff in 1996. Its keeper's house was moved in 1998.

The lighthouses are part of Cape Cod National Seashore. The grounds are open all year. Tours are given on an irregular schedule during spring and summer.

Moved back from the eroded beach cliffs of Eastham, Cape Cod, in 1996, Nauset Beach Light now stands on safe ground in Cape Cod National Seashore. The relocation came just in time. Only a few years later, the tower's original foundation tumbled into the waves. *Photograph by Shirin Pagels*

The nation's only set of triple light towers stood on Cape Cod. The Three Sisters, as sailors called them, were easily differentiated from the twin lights at Chatham and the single light at Truro. (**Top:** *Photograph from the Coast Guard Archives*) But by the 1980s, they were no longer used and in poor condition. (**Bottom:** *Photograph by Elinor De Wire*). The National Park Service rescued the lighthouses, refurbished them, and created a park where they now are displayed.

# Ned Point Lighthouse
## MATTAPOISETT

**FOR MORE INFORMATION**
www.lighthouse.cc/nedspoint/
index.html

**HOURS OF OPERATION**
A local Coast Guard auxiliary opens the tower for tours from 10:00 AM until noon on Thursdays in July and August. The grounds are open year-round.

**DIRECTIONS**
From MA 6 in Mattapoisett, drive south on North Street. At the terminus, turn left on Water Street, which becomes Beacon Street and then Ned Point Road, which ends at the lighthouse.

The rustic 1838 Ned Point Lighthouse features a rare hand-hewn, cantilevered granite stairway of thirty-two steps. Most early New England lighthouses had wooden steps. Iron stairways came into use circa 1850. *Photograph by Elinor De Wire*

The rubble-stone tower was built in 1838. Its tiny birdcage-style lantern exhibited a Lewis light with eleven whale-oil lamps and reflectors. The beacon shone from 41 feet above sea. While most lighthouses of the day had wooden stairways, Ned Point had thirty-two hand-hewn granite steps. A stone dwelling was attached to the tower by a covered walkway.

In 1857, a larger octagonal lantern equipped with a fifth-order Fresnel lens was installed. The dwelling was replaced in 1888 with a spacious two-story clapboard house. Eight years later, a third lantern was installed on the tower.

The station lost importance for navigation during the early twentieth century. In 1923, the house was taken by barge across Buzzards Bay to nearby Wings Neck Lighthouse. The tower was automated and continued to operate until 1952, at which time it was decommissioned. It was sold to the town of Mattapoisett a few years later.

A park was established around the lighthouse, which in 1961 was reactivated with a small light for nostalgia's sake. In 1995, renovations were completed and interpretive signs were added.

# Newburyport Harbor Range Lights
## NEWBURYPORT

This harbor is near the mouth of the Merrimack River and was an important fishing and lumber port during the 1800s. Range lights were established in 1873 to guide ships in the river channel, helping them avoid Goose Rocks. The front-range light was a 15-foot iron tower on Bayley's Wharf. The rear-range light shone from a 32-foot brick tower located 350 feet behind the wharf.

In 1901, both towers were elevated. They were taken out of service in 1961. The front-range tower was moved to a Coast Guard station, and the rear range was sold to private owners. The towers are not open to the public, but special dinners are sometimes held in the rear-range tower.

**FOR MORE INFORMATION**
Lighthouse Preservation Society
4 Middle Street
Newburyport, MA 01950
800.727.2326

**DIRECTIONS**
From I-95, take MA 133 to Water Street. The rear range is between Fair Street and Fruit Street. The front range sits at the Coast Guard station waterfront.

The range lights that once marked the Merrimack River channel stand in the small town of Newburyport. The rear light is a tall brick tower situated 350 feet behind the shorter front light on Bayley's Wharf. The beacons were deactivated in 1961.
*Photograph by Jeremy D'Entremont*

# Nobska Lighthouse
## WOODS HOLE

**FOR MORE INFORMATION**
United States Coast Guard
Auxilary
http://a01311.uscgaux.info/light
house_tours.html

**DIRECTIONS**
Take MA 28 south on Cape
Cod to Falmouth. Turn left on
Shore Street, which becomes
Surf Drive and then Oyster
Pond Road. Bear left onto
Nobska Road. There is a small
parking area by the lighthouse.

The lighthouse was established in 1828 to guide fishing vessels entering Falmouth. It was a cottage-style sentinel with a wooden tower rising from the roof of a stone house. Ten whale-oil lamps and reflectors supplied the beacon. Improvements were done in 1849, and a fifth-order lens was installed during the 1850s, but in 1876 the station was completely reconstructed. A 40-foot cast-iron tower lined with brick went into service beside a handsome Victorian keeper's dwelling. There was also a fogbell at the station. The lens was changed to a fourth-order apparatus in 1888.

New England's last civilian lightkeeper, Joseph Hindley, retired from this station in 1973. The Coast Guard crew left in 1985 when the lighthouse was automated. The keeper's residence became the home of the commander of the Coast Guard group at Woods Hole. The lighthouse grounds are open to the public every day. A local Coast Guard auxiliary occasionally opens the tower for tours.

Home to the commander of Coast Guard Group Woods Hole, Nobska Lighthouse flashes white every six seconds and shows a red sector to warn vessels off dangerous shoals. *Photograph by Elinor De Wire*

# Palmer's Island Lighthouse
## New Bedford

This lighthouse, built in 1849, is on a small island in the Acushnet River, and it marks the west side of the entrance to New Bedford Harbor. The 24-foot stone tower operated with whale-oil lamps and reflectors and a fogbell. It was connected to a wooden keeper's residence by an elevated walkway. In 1857, the lantern was upgraded with a fifth-order Fresnel lens. From 1888 to 1891, a red beacon on a nearby bridge worked in tandem with the lighthouse to provide a range for ships entering the harbor. A new fogbell was installed in 1900, and in 1904 an oil house was built to store kerosene.

**DIRECTIONS**
From I-195 in New Bedford, take exit 15 and drive south on MA 18. Then take Water Street to Union Street and make a left, and then turn right on Frontage Road. Look for signs for Twin Pier. The lighthouse is visible from the front of the hurricane wall.

The fierce 1938 hurricane destroyed the dwelling and boathouse and killed the keeper's wife. Repairs were made, and the station was automated in 1941. Completion of a hurricane barrier made the lighthouse obsolete in 1963. It was vandalized and set on fire. In 1978, a local group cleaned up the site and raised money to install a new lantern, stairway, and door. Vandalism continued, but in 1999 the city restored the lighthouse as a millennium project. A complete facelift and a new beacon returned much of the old sentinel's original splendor. The tower is not open to the public but can be seen distantly from New Bedford shore points, from the hurricane barrier, or from the ferry that runs from New Bedford to Cuttyhunk.

The infamous September 21, 1938, hurricane hit hard in Southern New England. Palmer's Island Light survived the storm, but all other buildings on the station were destroyed. Worse, the keeper was badly injured and his wife drowned. *Photograph from the author's collection*

# Plum Island Lighthouse
## NEWBURYPORT

**FOR MORE INFORMATION**
Friends of Plum Island
Lighthouse
P.O. Box 381
Newburyport, MA 01950

**DIRECTIONS**
From I-95, follow Route
113/1A into Newburyport and
take a left on Rolfe Lane, then
turn right onto the Plum
Island Turnpike. After crossing
the bridge to the island, take
the second left onto Northern
Boulevard and continue to the
lighthouse.

In 1787, range lights were established on the north end of the island at the entrance to the Merrimack River. These wooden towers guided ships into the river channel. The lights were feeble lamps fueled by whale oil. They were easy to move when erosion threatened. In 1790, the lights were ceded to the new federal government.

The lights were toppled by a tornado in 1808 and then rebuilt the following year. Extensive repairs were made to the towers in 1838. One of the lights burned down in 1856. The remaining sentinel was given a fourth-order Fresnel lens. By this time, a small beacon called the Bug Light had been added to the site. The towers were moved several times due to erosion before a new wooden lighthouse replaced them in 1898. The lens, fueled by kerosene, was relocated to the new tower. It was electrified in 1927 and automated in 1951.

For a few years, the keeper's dwelling was occupied by a ranger from Parker River National Wildlife Refuge. The lighthouse was given to the city of Newburyport in 2003 and is maintained by the Friends of Plum Island Lighthouse. They sporadically open it for tours during the summer. The grounds are open all year.

Newburyport, Mass. - Plum Island Light

Plum Island has had several light towers on its site to mark the dangerous entrance to the Merrimack River. An old post-card shows one of the 1838 range lights. Even with beacons to guide them, ships still wrecked. In 1839, the *Pocahontas* piled up on a sandbar during a storm, with the loss of all aboard. The tragedy was recorded in a poem by a famous New England poet and daughter of a lightkeeper, Celia Thaxter. *Photograph from the author's collection*

# Plymouth Lighthouse
## PLYMOUTH

A long sandy peninsula encloses Plymouth Harbor. The strip of land—named the Gurnet after a type of fish that was plentiful in the Pilgrim's native land—received its first lighthouse in 1769. The station consisted of a wooden house with lanterns rising from either end. It was the first twin-light station in America. In 1776, it earned the distinction of

**FOR MORE INFORMATION**
Project Gurnet and Bug Lights
P.O. Box 2167
Duxbury, MA 02331
www.buglight.org

having the first woman lightkeeper in the colonies when Hannah Thomas took over the station after her husband left to serve in the Revolutionary War.

The twin towers were transferred to the federal government in 1790. They were destroyed by fire in 1801 and then rebuilt in 1803, at which time the twins were separated. The small wooden sentinels stood 30 feet apart, with a keeper's dwelling nearby. They exhibited oil lamps and reflectors.

In 1843, a third set of twin lights was built. Two 34-foot octagonal wooden towers were connected by a short covered walkway. During the 1850s, they were improved with sixth-order Fresnel lenses. In 1871, they were upgraded with fourth-order lenses.

In 1924, the northeast twin was decommissioned and torn down. Later, a new dwelling was built. It was occupied until 1986 when the light was automated. The fourth-order lens was moved to the Hull Lifesaving Museum, and in 1989 the lighthouse site was leased to the U.S. Lighthouse Society. The keeper's dwelling became

a vacation rental. In 1998, when the society feared that erosion would claim the lighthouse, it was moved back from the sea to a new foundation. In 1999, the lease was transferred to Project Gurnet and Bug Lights. The group continues to maintain the station, which it opens to the public for an annual one-day open house during Duxbury's Opening of the Bay festival in May. The Gurnet sand spit is not open to the general public.

There was no light on the sand spit enclosing Plymouth Harbor in 1620 when the Pilgrims arrived, but in 1768 the tip of the spit was marked with twin lights. A succession of twin towers were built and rebuilt but were finally abandoned during the 1920s. Today the light on the Gurnet, the sand spit enclosing Plymouth Harbor, is a surviving twin built in 1843. *Photograph by Elinor De Wire*

# Point Gammon Lighthouse
## West Yarmouth

Warning of the dangerous rocks known as Bishops and Clerks, this field-stone lighthouse was built in 1816 to guide ships into Hyannis Harbor. Whale-oil lamps and reflectors provided the beacon. By the 1850s, the light was insufficient, and a temporary lightship was anchored near Bishop and Clerks. The lightship was replaced by a lighthouse on the rocks in 1858.

The lighthouse was ultimately sold to private owners, and the keeper's dwelling was torn down. The tower passed through several hands, then became a summer cottage for a time during the 1970s. The island is still privately owned and is off-limits to the public. The lighthouse is not open or accessible to the public and is best seen by boat.

Point Gammon Light at Hyannis had a short career of only forty-two years. It was too short and too distant from the busy shipping lanes of Cape Cod's south shore to be effective. In 1855, lightkeeper John Peak recorded 6,640 large vessels passing the station. A few years later, the beacon was transferred to the new Bishop and Clerks Lighthouse, which stood on a rock ledge in Nantucket Sound. Photograph by Shirin Pagels

# Race Point Lighthouse
## PROVINCETOWN

Built in 1816 to mark the perilous bar off the northern tip of Cape Cod, this short stone tower had a revolving Lewis light. A dwelling and a barn stood near the tower. Keepers accessed the station by walking or riding several miles over the sand. The station received a fogbell in 1852 and a fourth-order Fresnel lens in 1855. A steam fog signal replaced the bell during the 1970s.

A new 45-foot cast-iron lighthouse and two dwellings were built at this site in 1876. One residence was torn down in 1960 after the Coast Guard electrified the station. In 1978, the station was automated and the Fresnel lens was removed. Then the buildings were boarded up and stood empty for twenty years.

In 1995, the station underwent an amazing overhaul when the American Lighthouse Foundation began restoration. The dwelling was converted into a vacation rental operated by solar power. For a few years, the fog signal building served as a place to conduct marine mammal research. For rental reservations and four-wheel-drive access, call 508.487.9930.

**FOR MORE INFORMATION**
American Lighthouse Foundation
P.O. Box 889
Wells, ME 04090
207.646.0245
www.racepointlighthouse.net

**DIRECTIONS**
Drive north on MA 6 near Provincetown, watching for signs for Race Point Beach. The lighthouse is about a 45-minute hike from the beach parking area.

Laundry flapped on a clothesline at Race Point Light in a 1905 postcard scene. (**Left:** *Photograph from the author's collection*). In recent years, the keeper's house was converted to a vacation cottage, but the tower still operates as a navigational aid for vessels rounding the northern tip of Cape Cod. (**Right:** *Photograph by Elinor De Wire*)

# Sandy Neck Lighthouse
## BARNSTABLE

This lighthouse was established in 1826 on a long finger of sand enclosing the harbor at Barnstable. It guided whaling ships and other fishing traffic, especially during the stormy winter months. The lighthouse tower was incorporated into the roof of the keeper's dwelling. Ten lamps and reflectors provided the fixed white light.

A new brick lighthouse was built in 1857 with a Fresnel lens. The keeper's residence was rebuilt in 1880. After the tower developed cracks, it was stabilized around the middle with two iron hoops and staves. Changes in the shoreline rendered the lighthouse useless by 1931. Its lantern was removed, and the beacon was transferred to a steel skeleton tower that continued to serve until 1952. Sandy Neck Lighthouse has a new lantern, which was relighted on October 21, 2007. The lighthouse property was sold and is still in private hands. It is not open to the public and is best seen by boat.

After it was decommissioned in 1931, Sandy Neck Light's lantern was removed, and it was sold to a local family. During its active years, the lighthouse was an important sentinel for vessels plying Cape Cod Bay. Ice was a constant threat in the bay during winter months, and Sandy Neck's lightkeepers were kept busy assisting crews whose ships seized up in the ice. One keeper was killed after being pinned between an ice floe and his dory. *Photograph by Kraig Anderson*

# Sankaty Head Lighthouse
## NANTUCKET

The word *Sankaty* comes from a Native American word meaning "headland." It was on a 90-foot bluff on the southeast side of Nantucket near Siasconset that this lighthouse went into service in 1850. The 70-foot brick tower held a second-order Fresnel lens, the first in New England. A comfortable keeper's dwelling stood nearby, but it was not large enough to house the assistant keepers, who lived some distance away and traveled to the station by horse. A larger house was added in 1887.

Soon after its construction, the tower was painted with a broad red stripe to distinguish it from other sentinels in the area. In 1933, it was electrified, and a few years later the Coast Guard replaced the Victorian dwelling with a ranch-style duplex. Personnel lived in the duplex until 1992, despite the station's automation in 1965. The lantern was replaced in 1970.

Erosion slowly consumed the bluff and threatened the lighthouse. Thankfully, measures to slow the erosion were successful. However, a group called Save Our Sankaty attempted unsuccessfully to raise money to relocate the lighthouse away from the cliff. Sconset Trust has since raised money to move the lighthouse, which took up its new safe position in September 2007. The tower is not open to the public, but the grounds are open and accessible. The lens is displayed at the Nantucket Whaling Museum.

*Guardian of the deadly Nantucket Shoals, Sankaty Head Light wears a sash of red to distinguish it from neighboring sentinels. The 1850 sentinel holds the distinction of being the first lighthouse in the nation to have a Fresnel lens as part of its original lighting apparatus. The historic second-order lens was removed in 1950 and put on display at Nantucket Whaling Museum. A modern aerobeacon now operates in the lantern. Photograph by Shirin Pagels*

# Scituate Lighthouse
## SCITUATE

**FOR MORE INFORMATION**
Scituate Historical Society
P.O. Box 276
Scituate, MA 02066
781.545.1083
www.scituatehistorialsociety.org

**DIRECTIONS**
Driving north on MA 3A, turn right on First Parish Road toward Scituate Center. Watch for Beaverdam Road at a Y. Follow Beaverdam to Jericho Road and turn left, and then follow Jericho Road as it bears right onto Lighthouse Road.

In 1811, a 35-foot stone lighthouse was built on Cedar Point to guide fishing vessels into Scituate Harbor. A keeper's dwelling stood nearby. The lantern exhibited whale-oil lamps. The tower was heightened to 50 feet in 1827, and its beacon was converted to a piggyback design with a white light over a red light. The beacons were too close together, so the design was not successful, and in 1841 a Lewis light replaced the beacons.

Construction of Minots Ledge Lighthouse in 1850 made the Scituate Light unnecessary. It was extinguished for only a year when Minots Ledge toppled in a storm. The Scituate tower was relit until a new lighthouse was built on Minots Ledge in 1860. It then stood empty until 1890, at which time the completion of a breakwater at Cedar Point resulted in the erection of a small steel tower on the end of the wall. The steel-tower keeper took up residence at the lighthouse, but the Scituate Light remained dark.

The lighthouse was sold to the town of Scituate in 1917. Today it is rented out by the town as a private residence. A park surrounds the lighthouse, which was relit in 1994. The tower is open for tours on select days. Contact the Scituate Historical Society for dates. The grounds are open year-round.

Famous for the "Army of Two," Scituate Lighthouse was saved from attack during the War of 1812 by the clever daughters of lightkeeper Simeon Bates. Teenagers Abigail and Rebecca Bates were alone at the lighthouse when British soldiers rowed ashore from a warship. The girls grabbed their little brother's fife and drum, hid behind a sand dune, and began playing martial music. The soldiers thought the town militia was approaching and quickly withdrew. *Photograph by Elinor De Wire*

# Stage Harbor Lighthouse
## CHATHAM

A 48-foot cast-iron lighthouse was built in 1880 at a cost of $10,000 to mark Chatham Roads, the waterway into Stage Harbor. It exhibited a fifth-order Fresnel lens. The tower was connected to a two-story dwelling by a covered walkway. The sentinel served until 1933, at which time a smaller beacon on a steel tower replaced it. The lantern was removed from the tower and was sold to a private family. The station has never been modernized with electricity or plumbing. It is not open to the public and is best seen by boat.

A guide for vessels traveling the Chatham Roads, Stage Harbor Light served from 1880 until 1933. When it was deactivated and replaced in 1933 by an automatic light on a skeleton tower, the keeper complained bitterly to a *Boston Post* reporter: "to save money they put in something that is far more expensive and less reliable, and all that economy put another employee on the unemployment list. Rather a poor way to reduce unemployment and surely no help toward better times." *Photograph by Kraig Anderson*

# Straitsmouth Island Lighthouse
## ROCKPORT

Despite a thriving granite industry in Rockport, the lighthouse that guided ships into Pigeon Cove was built of brick. The 19-foot tower, constructed in 1835, was connected to a spacious brick keeper's dwelling by an open walkway. In 1851, the lighthouse was completely rebuilt as an octagonal stone tower 24 feet tall. A sixth-order Fresnel lens was installed in 1857, and a new wooden dwelling was built in 1878. In 1896, a third lighthouse was constructed. The cylindrical brick tower was 37 feet tall and was fueled by kerosene.

The island was sold to a private party in 1941. The station continued in operation and was automated in 1967. By this time, the island was owned by the National Audubon Society. Though the tower is maintained by the Coast Guard, the dwelling has deteriorated. Neither the lighthouse nor Straitsmouth Island are open to the public.

Not every lighthouse can be saved from eventual demise. Straitsmouth Island Light has been vacant since the 1930s, and evidence of its neglect is readily apparent. Efforts to restore the aging keeper's house have been thwarted by vandalism, bad weather, and rats and seabirds living inside it. A storm in October 1991 seriously damaged the tower. *Photograph by Shirin Pagels*

# Tarpaulin Cove Lighthouse
## GOSNOLD

This lighthouse was built in 1817 to replace a private light on a tavern. It sat on Naushon Island, one of a group of islands that extends southwest from Cape Cod and encloses Buzzards Bay. The 38-foot stone lighthouse had ten lamps and reflectors. A fifth-order Fresnel lens was installed in 1856, and a new keeper's dwelling was built in 1888, fol-

**FOR MORE INFORMATION**
Cuttyhunk Historical Society
P.O. Box 165
Cuttyhunk, MA 02713
508.971.0932

lowed by a new 28-foot brick lighthouse in 1891. The lens was upgraded to a fourth-order Fresnel, and a fogbell was added. The bell was a casualty of the 1938 hurricane.

In 1941, the station was automated. It deteriorated, and all but the light tower was razed in 1961. A modern beacon now shines from the tower. It is in the care of the Cuttyhunk Historical Society but is not open to the public. It is best seen by boat, since Naushon Island is privately owned.

Chickens forage on the lawn at Tarpaulin Cove Lighthouse circa 1920. The family living there also probably had a cow and a horse. Most lightkeepers kept livestock in order to maintain a small measure of self-sufficiency.
*Photograph from the Coast Guard Archives*

# Ten Pound Island Lighthouse
## GLOUCESTER

**DIRECTIONS**

Drive east on MA 127 in Gloucester, cross the Annisquam River Bridge, and follow it onto Stacey Blvd. The lighthouse is visible to the right in the harbor.

A 20-foot stone lighthouse was established in 1821 in Gloucester Harbor on an island rumored to have been named for its price, paid by colonists to the local natives. The more likely explanation is that ten pens (pounds) for sheep were once located on the island. A stone keeper's house was connected to the tower by a covered walkway. The lantern held ten oil lamps and reflectors. These were replaced by a fifth-order Fresnel lens during the 1850s. In 1881, the crumbling tower was replaced by a new 30-foot cast-iron lighthouse. A new wooden dwelling also was built at this time.

The station was closed in 1956, and the beacon was moved to the bell tower. Later, a skeleton tower took its place. During the 1980s, the Lighthouse Preservation Society raised $40,000 to refurbish the lighthouse. The beacon was returned to the lantern on August 7, 1989—the bicentennial of the U.S. Lighthouse Establishment. The lighthouse is not open to the public but can be seen from numerous points along the Gloucester waterfront and from area boat cruises.

An old-style birdcage lantern adorned the original Ten Pound Island Lighthouse, built in 1821 at Gloucester. Named for its resemblance to a birdcage, the lantern had small windows and an iron superstructure to protect the keeper as he cleaned the exterior. With the advent of large prism lenses during the 1840s, birdcage lanterns disappeared, since they were not big enough to accommodate the lenses. *Photograph from the Coast Guard Archives*

# Thacher Island Twin Lighthouses
## ROCKPORT

Thatcher Island was named for Anthony Thacher, whose ship wrecked on it in 1635. In 1771, twin 45-foot stone lighthouses, located 300 yards apart and flanking a stone keeper's dwelling, were constructed to assist ships passing dangerous Londoner Ledge. The original light source was most likely tallow candles. Sailors soon nicknamed the twin towers Ann's Eyes, since they stood watch off Cape Ann. In 1810, the south tower was equipped with an Argand lamp. A new dwelling was built four years later. Both towers were given Lewis lights in 1841, and about this same time a new keeper's house was constructed. A fogbell was added in 1853.

In 1861, new granite light towers were built, each 124 feet tall and housing first-order Fresnel lenses. A new wooden keeper's dwelling was erected near the north tower. In 1876, a second dwelling was built near the south tower. The lights continued in service until 1932, at which time the north light was deactivated and the south light was intensified.

In 1982, the beacon was automated and the lens was replaced by a modern optic. The old lens is now on display at the Coast Guard Academy Museum. A non-profit group has renovated the houses and the towers and offers limited access to them. The Thacher Island Launch, only for members of the Thacher Island Association, runs to the island at 9:00 AM on Saturday mornings in July and August. Reservations are required to ride the launch, to rent rooms in the old dwelling, or to camp on the island.

**FOR MORE INFORMATION**
P.O. Box 73
Rockport, MA 01966
978.546.7697 (for launch information)
617.599.2590 (for camping and overnight stays)

**DIRECTIONS**
Drive south from Rockport on MA 127A and take a right on Penryn Way to Penzance Road. Follow Penzance Road to Old Penzance Road. The lights are visible about a mile offshore.

The south tower of the Thacher Island Twin Lights still operates using solar power. *Photograph by Shirin Pagels*

# TWINS, TRIPLETS, AND RANGES

*As the tide came, the sea rose higher and higher, till the only endurable places were*
*the light-towers. If they stood we were saved, otherwise our fate was only too certain.*
Abbie Burgess, Keeper's Daughter
Matinicus Rock Twin Lights

Abbie Burgess wrote these words in her logbook about the worst day of the great nor'easter in January 1856. She lived at an unusual light station. Matinicus Rock had twin lights—two towers, two beacons, one house. It was a design found primarily in New England. But why would a light station require two towers?

Some harbor and river stations had range lights, or two towers situated one above the other. The lower light was situated nearest to shore and was called the front range; the higher light sat back from shore and was called the rear range. The purpose of range lights was to help ships stay on course in tricky channels leading into harbors and rivers. A navigator steered until the lights were lined up one over the other and then proceeded into the channel. Newburyport Harbor had one of the earliest ranges, built in 1787 to guide vessels into the Merrimack River.

But a station like Matinicus was far from shore. Its twin lights—two towers situated a short distance apart—served a different function. Until about 1850, these multiple lights were the only option available in the United States to differentiate coastal lighthouses situated near each other. In places like Maine and Massachusetts, where lighthouses were heavily concentrated, mariners easily could become disoriented. By 1820, some locations along the New England coast had as many as nine coastal lights in view at once. All the beacons were white and fixed. Unless a navigator knew the shoreline like the back of his hand, he could easily become confused.

The solution was to build multiple lights in problem areas. This practice was borrowed from Europe, where similar coastlines exhibited multiple lights. The first location to receive twin lights in America was Plymouth in 1769, followed by Thacher Island off Cape Ann in 1771. The Massachusetts Bay Colony feared ships making landfall at Boston might mistake the lights at these sites for the Boston Light. Navigational instruments and methods were not sophisticated at this time, and making landfall was a great challenge. By setting up twin lights on both sites, Plymouth and Cape Ann were easier to identify.

Twin lights also were built on Block Island in Rhode Island, on Baker's Island off Gloucester, in Chatham on Cape Cod, and at Cape Elizabeth and Matinicus Rock in Maine. The only twin-light station outside New England was built at Navesink, New Jersey.

A unique triple-light station went into service on Cape Cod in 1838 at Eastham. Here, inshore vessels needed a guiding beacon that looked different from the twin lights at Chatham to the south or the single light at Truro to the north. The Three Sisters of Nauset, as sailors affectionately dubbed them, were a trio of small wooden towers sitting in a row on the bluffs of Nauset. From sea, they resembled three little ladies in white dresses and black hats. They were the only triple lights ever built in the United States.

Experimental piggyback light systems also were used in some lighthouses. Scituate Light in

A method of distinguishing lights in the years before flashing beacons were devised was to build multiple towers and beacons. Matinicus Rock, Maine, had twin lights—two towers meant twice the work for the keepers. An image from the 1890s shows the keepers with their families.
*Photograph from the Coast Guard Archives*

Massachusetts had this type of apparatus, as did Rhode Island's old North Light on Block Island. The beacons were located in a single tower, one positioned above the other and each a different color. These piggyback systems proved ineffective, however, because their beams merged only a short distance offshore and appeared as a single light. The red light, which has a much shorter range (that is, the distance it can be seen) than the white light, failed to show more than a few miles.

By 1850, the Fresnel lens was introduced to American lighthouses, and its signaling capability rendered all types of multiple lights unnecessary. A single Fresnel beacon could be made to flash, occult, or vary its colors in a variety of patterns. The navigator needed only to memorize the light signals or to consult a light list to know which beacon he was seeing.

The Fresnel lens rendered twin and triple lights useless, but they continued to serve into the 1920s. Nostalgia and public insistence was to blame. After the 1850s, the U.S. Lighthouse Board knew full well it was overlighting the coasts of Maine and Massachusetts, but tradition often dies slowly. All twin and triple lights were fitted with Fresnel lenses by 1870. Cape Elizabeth's twin lights at Portland were typical of the redundancy of light: one flashed, and the other showed a fixed light. A single flashing light would have sufficed.

Range lights still serve in many areas in New England. Their lights are not redundant, since their purpose is different from that of twin and triple lights. Piggyback beacons were discontinued by 1900. Twin lights were gone by 1935, but twin towers remain standing at Matinicus Rock, Cape Elizabeth, and Cape Ann. (Navesink, New Jersey, still has its twin towers as well.)

The defunct Matinicus twin lost its lantern after its sister was automated in 1983. Cape Elizabeth's twins are no longer identical, due to the sale of one of the twins to a private family during the 1930s and its subsequent remodeling. Thacher Island retains its historic twins, looking much as they did a century ago, but only one is lit. The retired Three Sisters of Nauset are now charming showpieces on Cape Cod National Seashore. Two are missing their lanterns, removed in 1923 when the lighthouses were sold to private individuals. The whereabouts of the two missing lanterns are unknown.

# West Chop Lighthouse
## MARTHA'S VINEYARD

**DIRECTIONS**
From the ferry slip, take Union Street and then turn right on Main Street, which becomes West Chop Road and leads to the lighthouse.

A light has shined over Vineyard Haven since 1817, when a 25-foot stone tower was built on the west shore. Oil lamps and reflectors provided the beacon, and a simple keeper's dwelling stood nearby. The station was rebuilt in 1846, almost a fifth of a mile away. A few years later, three range lights were built in the harbor, but they proved unnecessary and were deactivated in 1859. By then, the tower had a fourth-order Fresnel lens. A steam fog signal was added to the station in 1872.

A new lighthouse was built in 1891 after the development of a summer resort in the area interfered with the beacon. The 45-foot brick tower started out red but was changed to white in 1896. Families continued to serve at the station until it was automated in 1976. The lens remained in place. A Coast Guard family currently lives in one of the dwellings. The tower is not open and the grounds are private, but the lighthouse can be seen easily from the road.

Comely West Chop Lighthouse operates a classical fourth-order Fresnel lens and signals to vessels entering and leaving Vineyard Haven Harbor. The white light occults every four seconds and shows a red sector to warn of dangerous shoals. The house serves as quarters for the commanding officer of Coast Guard station Menemsha. *Photograph by Kraig Anderson*

# Wings Neck Lighthouse
## POCASSET

The first lighthouse at this site was built in 1848 to guide ships through Buzzards Bay. The 38-foot sentinel was a cottage-style design, with the tower rising from the roof of the dwelling. It exhibited whale-oil lamps with reflectors but was equipped with a small Fresnel lens in 1856. Fire damaged the station during the 1870s.

The station was rebuilt entirely in 1890. The new wooden lighthouse was hexagonal in shape. The keeper's house was built at the same time, and a walkway was added later to connect the house to the tower. In 1923, the keeper's house at Ned Point Light was moved to Wings Neck to serve as a home for an assistant keeper. The station was decommissioned in 1945 after the opening of Cleveland Ledge Light. It was sold to a private family. The lighthouse is not open to the public, but the house is available for rent.

**FOR MORE INFORMATION**
Wings Neck Lighthouse Trust
508.430.8685
www.wingsnecklighthouse.com
admin@wingsnecklighthouse.com

**DIRECTIONS**
From MA 28 near Pocasset, drive west on Barlows Landing Road. Cross Shore Road and bear right on Wings Neck Road. The lighthouse can be seen from a gate at the end of this road.

Wings Neck Lighthouse served ships on Buzzards Bay from 1890 until 1945. Among its most famous keepers were brothers George and William Howard, who served together during the 1920s and 1930s and who saved many lives. Their father had been the captain of the Cross Rip Lightship in Vineyard Sound, and the brothers learned skillful boat-handling abilities. William Howard is said to have saved more than thirty-five people during his career. *Photograph from Wings Neck Light Trust*

# Wood End Lighthouse
## PROVINCETOWN

**FOR MORE INFORMATION**
American Lighthouse
Foundation
P.O. Box 889
Wells, ME 04090
207.646.0245
www.lighthousefoundation.org
info@lighthousefoundation.org

**DIRECTIONS**
See directions to Long Point
Lighthouse.

A daymark led ships into Provincetown Harbor as early as 1864. It was replaced in 1872 by a 39-foot square brick lighthouse flanked by a wood-frame dwelling. The tower was painted brown and exhibited a fifth-order Fresnel lens. By 1902, the station had a new dwelling, an oil house, and a fogbell. A revolving light was installed in 1900.

After automation in 1961, the Coast Guard razed everything but the tower. It was solarized in 1981. The tower is licensed to the American Lighthouse Foundation, which has made some improvements to it. It is not open to the public, but the grounds can be accessed via a long hike from Provincetown.

Little Wood End Light near Provincetown flashes red once every ten seconds. Other than the tower, the only structure remaining on the site is the oil house, a tidy brick building where incendiary kerosene was stored before the station was electrified. Today solar power runs the light. *Photograph by Elinor De Wire*

# Poets and Painters

*The lighthouse was built upon these cruel treacherous wave-beaten rocks. Boulders and stones, some worn down with time and tide; slippery, loose of their foundations.*
Ruth Carmen
*Storm Child*, 1937

Ruth Carmen was inspired to pen *Storm Child* after meeting little Georgia Norwood, the youngest of child of Boston Light keeper Ralph Norwood. Georgia's good looks and cloistered life at the light station were just the grist Carmen needed for a searing drama. Georgia's birth in 1932 also had a traumatic storm story associated with it. The book sold well, sent Georgia and her mother on a national tour, and inspired Hollywood producers.

Author Ruth Carmen found grist for a good novel in the true tale of the Norwood family's service at Boston Light during the 1930s and of the birth of their daughter Georgia during a horrific storm. *Storm Child* sold well and propelled the reclusive family into a short but bittersweet period of fame. *Photograph from the author's collection*

Lighthouses seem to enchant writers, painters, poets, playwrights, and film producers. Eugene O'Neill was emotionally affected by the lighthouses around his home in New London, Connecticut, and incorporated them into his plays. The sorrowful wailing of the foghorn on Ledge Light became a repetitious reminder of addictions and misery in *Long Day's Journey into Night*. O'Neill likened the omnipresent horn to a "mournful whale in labor."

Henry Wadsworth Longfellow was consumed by metaphors of the lighthouse. Many of his poems center on the theme of shipwreck and disaster, but he was also aware of the majesty of lighthouses. His famous poem "The Lighthouse" was written on the rocks below Portland Head Light circa 1845 and captures in words what many of us strive to record with a camera: "Steadfast, serene, immoveable . . . through all the silent night burns on forever more that quenchless flame."

Celia Thaxter spent her childhood at White Island Light in the Isles of Shoals, New Hampshire. The isolation and simplicity of her life, punctuated by storms and disasters, was later captured in her poetry. She described seeing the lighthouse for the first time in 1839 as "a black-capped giant" looking down on her. The beacon was fascinating for the four-year-old, with its "rich red and golden" lamps swinging "around in mid-air."

Rudyard Kipling spent time at Annisquam Light in Massachusetts. He was an avid traveler and lover of the sea. Best known for his *Just So Stories* and *The Jungle Book*, Kipling was also a lighthouse fancier and wrote several poems and stories featuring sentinels, including his lyrical "Coastwise Lights."

Artists have always drawn inspiration from lighthouses. Edward Hopper is known for his subtle watercolor of Cape Elizabeth Light called *Two Lights*. It was featured on a U.S. Postal Service stamp during the 1980s. Winslow Homer included lighthouses in his seascapes, as did Andrew Wyeth and Jamie Wyeth, owners of Tenants Harbor Light in Maine.

Sir Edwin Henry Landseer was so taken with the courageous story of Milo, a lightkeeper's dog at Massachusetts' Egg Rock Light during the 1850s, he painted *Saved*. It shows a near-drowned boy sprawled on the huge dog's paws. The painting brought fame to the big Newfoundland–St. Bernard mix and underscored the dangers of working at a lighthouse. The irony of the painting became apparent a few years later when the boy drowned.

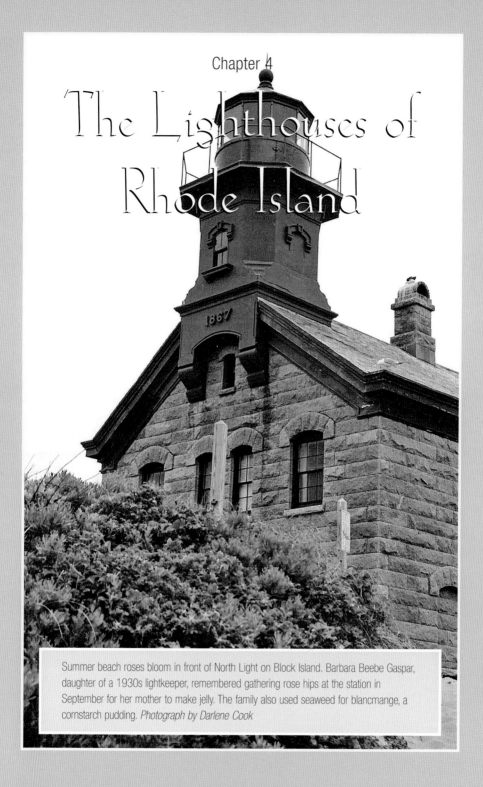

# Chapter 4
# The Lighthouses of Rhode Island

Summer beach roses bloom in front of North Light on Block Island. Barbara Beebe Gaspar, daughter of a 1930s lightkeeper, remembered gathering rose hips at the station in September for her mother to make jelly. The family also used seaweed for blancmange, a cornstarch pudding. *Photograph by Darlene Cook*

# Beavertail Lighthouse
## JAMESTOWN

A simple beacon was erected on the southern tip of Conanicut Island as early as 1712 to guide ships into Narragansett Bay. A fog cannon was set up in 1719, followed by a simple 58-foot wooden lighthouse in 1749. It was the third sentinel constructed in the colonies. The lamps caught fire in 1753, and the tower burned down. It was rebuilt but burned again in 1779, this time at the hands of British soldiers.

In 1856, a new lighthouse was built. The 45-foot square granite tower held a third-order Fresnel lens fueled by whale oil. A brick keeper's residence replaced the old stone house. By the 1880s, kerosene was used at the station, and in 1931 electricity came to the point. The station suffered damage during the 1938 hurricane, which also claimed the life of the keeper's daughter. Another storm rocked the station in 1954. The buildings were repaired, but the station had become costly to staff. It was automated in 1972.

**FOR MORE INFORMATION**
Beavertail Lighthouse Museum Association
P.O. Box 83
Jamestown, RI 02835
www.beavertaillight.org
info@beavertaillight.org

**DIRECTIONS**
From RI 138 on the east side of the Newport Bridge, drive to Jamestown Center. Continue south past Mackerel Cove Town Beach and follow signs to Beavertail State Park.

Beavertail Lighthouse was a testing station for fog signals, due to the Narragansett Bay's frequent dense fogs. A modern electric foghorn is seen on the platform in the fenced area at right, but earlier signals ranged from bells to whistles to trumpets and horns. The bellows for an 1850s fog trumpet was powered by a horse walking around a windlass. *Photograph by Elinor De Wire*

# Block Island North Lighthouse
## New Shoreham

**FOR MORE INFORMATION**
Block Island North Light
Association
P.O. Box 1662
Block Island, RI 02807
401.466.3200

**HOURS OF OPERATION**
Open weekends from 10:00
A.M. to 5:00 P.M. from
Memorial Day until the
island's famous sailboat Race
Week in late June, then daily
until Columbus Day.

**DIRECTIONS**
The lighthouse is accessible
by ferry from Point Judith,
Rhode Island, from New
London, Connecticut, or from
Montauk, New York. Once on
the island, the lighthouse can
be reached by car, bike, or taxi
via Corn Neck Road. Park in
the lot adjacent to the site and
walk over the sand spit to the
lighthouse.

Six lighthouses have stood on Sandy Point at the northern tip of the island. The first two, a wooden set of twin towers on the roof of the keeper's dwelling, went into service in 1829. They were replaced with a second set of rooftop twin lights in 1837, followed by a single granite tower in 1857. The current 55-foot granite lighthouse was built in 1868 to replace its deteriorated 1857 predecessor. It was an integral design with an iron tower on the roof of a granite keeper's dwelling. A fourth-order Fresnel lens was installed. Keepers accessed the station over a long sand spit on foot or by horseback. During the 1940s, the Coast Guard gave keepers of this light a Jeep. The lighthouse was automated in 1956 and was decommissioned in 1973 when the light was moved to a skeleton tower.

Block Island is an obstacle at the northern entrance to Long Island Sound. Over a period of twenty years in the early nineteenth century, sixty vessels wrecked on its shores. Losses were reduced greatly after the erection of a lighthouse in 1828. The current sentinel, affectionately known as Old Granitesides, was built in 1868.
*Photograph by Shirin Pagels*

# Block Island Southeast Lighthouse
## New Shoreham

A Gothic-style lighthouse was built on Mohegan Bluffs in 1875 to guide ships around the south side of the island and into Long Island Sound. The 52-foot brick tower was attached to a brick dwelling. Its first-order lens shone from 204 feet above sea level—the most elevated in New England. A steam fog signal served until 1908, when its building burned down. It was rebuilt and continued to operate until a modern electronic horn was installed in 1974.

A new first-order lens was installed in 1929. It revolved in a tub of mercury. The light was badly damaged during the 1938 hurricane, and the keepers had to turn it by hand for many days after the storm.

Erosion became the station's worst nemesis. Originally built 300 feet from the bluffs, it stood less than 75 feet from the bluffs when the light was decommissioned in 1990. The beacon was moved to a steel tower.

A nonprofit group raised money to have the tower moved back from the cliff in 1993. The mercury lens was removed and was replaced by a safer first-order lens from Cape Lookout Lighthouse in North Carolina. Block Island Southeast Lighthouse became a National Historic Landmark in 1997. A museum was established inside the lighthouse, and the beacon was relit. Museum hours vary.

**FOR MORE INFORMATION**
Block Island Southeast
Lighthouse Foundation
Box 949
Block Island, RI 02807
401.466.5009
selight@verizon.net

**DIRECTIONS**
The lighthouse is accessible by ferry from Point Judith, Rhode Island, from New London, Connecticut, or from Montauk, New York. Once on the island, the lighthouse can be reached on the southeast shore by car, bike, or taxi.

Moving lighthouses out of harm's way has become commonplace. Relocation of Block Island's Southeast Light was the first such effort in modern times. In August 1993, the 2,000-ton lighthouse was moved 300 feet back from the edge of Monhegan Bluffs. *Photograph by Elinor De Wire*

# Bristol Ferry Lighthouse
## BRISTOL

**DIRECTIONS**

Traveling north on RI 114 from Portsmouth, enter the town of Bristol Ferry and veer right onto Bristol Ferry Road at the intersection before the Mount Hope Bridge. Watch for signs for Bristol Ferry Wharf. The lighthouse can be seen distantly from the wharf.

Beginning in 1846, a private beacon was exhibited near the port of Bristol, where whaling ships and a ferry plied the foggy passage between Mount Hope Bay and Narragansett Bay. Despite repeated pleas from local merchants, a lighthouse was not built until 1855. The 28-foot brick tower was attached to a keeper's house and exhibited a sixth-order Fresnel lens fueled by whale-oil lamps. Several outbuildings were added to the station over the years, as well as a white picket fence during the 1870s.

The lighthouse was updated in 1902 with a fifth-order lens. A decade later, the rotting wooden lantern was replaced by an iron lantern from a defunct lighthouse in the Hudson River in New York. The station continued in service until 1927, at which time a steel skeleton tower took over its duties. A year later, the lantern was removed and the property was sold to a local family. It changed hands several times. During the late 1990s, the owners fabricated a new lantern for the tower and installed a low-intensity beacon. The lighthouse is a private home and is not open to the public. It can be seen beneath Mount Hope Bridge.

The lightkeeper posed beside his luminous charge in an 1870s photo of Bristol Ferry Lighthouse, marking the tricky passage between MountHope Bay and Narragansett Bay. The site was named for a ferry that once ran from Bristol to Aquidneck Island. *Photograph from the National Archives*

# Castle Hill Lighthouse
## NEWPORT

The rugged 34-foot granite tower was built into the rocks on the bank of the harbor in 1890. A fifth-order Fresnel lens flashed red from the iron lantern, and a fogbell hung from the seaward side. A short distance from the tower, a house for the keeper was nestled into Castle Hill Cove. The 1,300-pound fogbell's service was interrupted several times as a result of complaints from local residents. A larger bell went into service in 1896. Three years later, the upper half of the tower was painted with a white daymark to make it visible against the gray rocks behind it.

The station was automated in 1957, and its lens was replaced with a modern optic. The keeper's dwelling was sold to private owners. In 1992, the dilapidated wooden stairway was replaced by concrete steps. The lighthouse is not open to the public but can be viewed from a path leading from the parking area at the Inn at Castle Hill.

**DIRECTIONS**

In Newport, go south on America's Cup Avenue (which becomes Thames Avenue) and turn right on Wellington Avenue. Go left on Halidon Avenue, right on Harrison Avenue, right on Castle Hill Road, and left on Ocean Drive. Watch for a sign to the marina. Park opposite the marina and walk the path to the lighthouse.

Visitors tour rugged Castle Hill Light in Newport. The notch on the harbor side of the tower once held a fogbell. The bell is now on display at nearby Castle Hill Coast Guard Station. *Photograph by Elinor De Wire*

# Conanicut Island Lighthouse
## JAMESTOWN

C onanicut Island divides the Narragansett Bay into east and west passages. A lighthouse was established on the northern tip of the island in 1886 to assist southbound vessels as they chose one or the other passage. The square, white, wooden tower, 47 feet above sea level, was attached to a pretty Victorian dwelling. It was equipped with a fifth-order Fresnel lens. A fogbell was installed in a separate building.

In 1900, the bell was deactivated, and a fog siren took over its duties. By this time, the beacon had been given a red sector to mark a danger zone. By 1932, shipping traffic in the area had decreased. The U.S. Bureau of Lighthouses decided an automatic beacon on a skeleton tower would save money. The lantern on the lighthouse was removed and sold. The tower itself also was sold. Private owners later painted it red. The lighthouse is not open to the public and is not accessible.

Shorn of its lantern, the old sentinel at Conanicut Island bears little resemblance to a lighthouse. Its lantern was removed during the 1930s after it was deactivated. The structure sold at auction for $2,785 and remains privately owned. *Photograph by Jeremy D'Entremont*

# Conimicut Shoal Lighthouse
## WARWICK

A shoal extending from Conimicut Point in the middle of the entrance to the Providence River was marked with a daybeacon in 1858. It was replaced in 1866 by a stone lighthouse. At the same time, nearby Nayatt Point Light was decommissioned. Its keeper's house became the home of Conimicut's light-keepers for the next eight years. They rowed out to the tower each day to tend it.

In 1874, a dwelling was built on the landing pier at Conimicut Light. Only a year later, the new house was destroyed by ice floes on the river. Once again, lightkeepers were forced to live at the defunct Nayatt Point Light and row to Conimicut Light. The problem was solved in 1882 with the construction of a 58-foot cast-iron caisson lighthouse on the shoal. Its design included quarters for the keepers. It exhibited a fourth-order Fresnel lens, and a red sector marked Conimicut Middle Ground and guided vessels into the West Passage. The station also had a fogbell.

The tower was electrified in 1960 and was automated in 1963 with a modern optic. Ownership of the lighthouse was transferred to the city of Warwick in 2005, and the Conimicut Lighthouse Foundation was formed to care for it. The tower is not open to the public but can be seen by boat or from a park in Warwick.

**DIRECTIONS**
Travel north from Warwick on RI 117, turn right on Terrace Street, and then make a quick left onto Symonds Avenue. Turn right at Point Avenue and drive to Conimicut Point Park. The lighthouse is visible in the distance from the park shore.

The cast-iron caisson lighthouse at Conimicut Shoal near Barrington is typical of the many sparkplug-style sentinels in New England. Since its automation in 1963, the tower has become a refuge for seabirds. In 1997, a Coast Guard maintenance crew was surprised to find a coyote in the lighthouse. It had somehow swum to the light and become stranded. The men caged the frightened animal and took it to the mainland, where it was released into the wild.
*Photograph by Shirin Pagels*

# Dutch Island Lighthouse
## JAMESTOWN

Situated on an 81-acre island west of the larger Conanicut Island, this lighthouse was commissioned in 1827. The 30-foot slate stone tower, outfitted with a Lewis light, guided vessels through the treacherous West Passage of the Narragansett Bay and into Dutch Island Harbor. A tiny keeper's dwelling abutted the tower.

In 1857, after the first lighthouse was deemed "wretched" and the "worst constructed of any in the state" by the Lighthouse Board, it was replaced with a stronger 42-foot square brick tower painted with a white daymark. The lantern held a fourth-order lens. The island was frequently swathed in fog, so in 1878 a fogbell was installed on the exterior northwest wall of the lighthouse. Its melodious bongs were created by an automatic striker powered by clockworks.

The lighthouse was automated in 1947. In 1958, the island was deeded to the state of Rhode Island as a wildlife refuge. Though the birds on the island were protected, the lighthouse was not, and it began to deteriorate and suffered from vandalism. In 1960, everything but the tower and engine house was torn down. The beacon was deactivated in 1979 and was replaced by buoy lights in the passage. A nonprofit group formed in 2000 and, with the help of the American Lighthouse Foundation is attempting to restore the lighthouse. While the site is not open to the public, the tower can be seen in the distance from several places on the west side of Conanicut Island and from the Fort Getty Recreation Area in Jamestown.

The 1857 Dutch Island Lighthouse was a brick tower abutting the keeper's quarters. A man is shown standing on the foundation of the first tower, a 30-foot stone sentinel built in 1827. The site was named by the West India Company of Holland, which established a trading post on the 81-acre island during the 1630s. *Photograph from the American Lighthouse Foundation*

# THE LARDER AND LIVESTOCK

The U.S. Lighthouse Service supplied staple foods to light-keepers, especially at sites where no livestock could be raised or gardens planted. Sugar, flour, molasses, salted meat, potatoes, coffee, and beans were delivered by supply ship. Later, canned milk and an assortment of canned meats and vegetables were included. But families still had to augment their provisions in order to survive.

Gardens, where possible, were indispensable. Salt air was a bane, and sandy soil had to be enriched, but the yield was worth the effort. Fish often provided much-needed fertilizer. Even lightkeepers on rocky islets and at water-bound lighthouses had gardens, sometimes on windowsills. The lonely outposts at Saddleback Ledge and Mount Desert were known for their rock gardens. Their keepers hauled dirt to the stations each spring, crammed it into rock crevices, and planted vegetables and flowers. Autumn storms tore out the dirt, which had to be replenished the following spring.

At stations with sufficient pasture, it was not uncommon for keepers to have a cow. On the mainland, the cow was usually walked to the lighthouse or brought by wagon. At island stations, the cow was lightered across the water, pushed over-

Lightkeeper Elson Small had a gentle Jersey cow named Blossom at Maine's St. Croix River Lighthouse during the 1920s. The Coast Guard was so impressed with Small's tidy little lighthouse farm that they snapped a publicity photo of him milking Blossom to use for recruitment purposes. *Photograph from the American Lighthouse Foundation*

board, and swam to shore. It was a harrowing experience, but her value to the family was immeasurable as a source of milk, cream, and butter. At Matinicus Rock Light during the 1890s, a magazine reporter observed the station cow standing on a high point looking landward and occasionally giving out with a long, low bawl. "Daisy is sensibly affected by her environment," he glibly wrote. The only creature of her kind on the island, she was lonely beyond description.

Sheep were among the earliest lighthouse livestock. Boston Light's first keeper had a flock on Great Brewster Island for mutton and wool. They survived only a year before a 1717 storm sent the tide rushing over the island and drowned them. Sheep were also raised on Nash Island Light, and still live beneath the old tower as part of the interpretive history of the station.

Chickens were the most common livestock. They are mentioned in countless lighthouse records. Chicken coops usually were included in the design of a light station, and when they weren't, keepers improvised. At Gull Rocks Light in Narragansett Bay, chickens roosted in the rocks around the wave-swept tower. Keepers gathered their eggs, but sometimes storm waves took the eggs, which would later wash ashore in Newport, mystifying beach-combers.

Fish, lobster, oysters, and clams—readily available just outside the lighthouse door—were important in a keeper's diet. So were seabirds. When provisions ran low, it was often seabird eggs or the wayward duck slamming into the tower that put food on the table. The most fortuitous meal came one stormy November at desolate Boon Island Lighthouse, nine miles off southern Maine. Other than a few potatoes and onions, the keepers were nearly out of provisions with no chance to get ashore in the bad weather. On Thanksgiving Eve, a fat duck collided with the lantern and fell dead at the men's feet. The next day, the unfortunate fowl appeared on the kitchen table, accompanied by gamey gravy, boiled potatoes, and onions.

# The Great Equinoctial Storm

*She tried to bring succor to her mate,*
*who struggled in the raging tide.*
Obituary of Mabel Small
Lightkeeper's Wife, Palmer's Island Lighthouse

S torms assail lighthouses, no matter where a lighthouse stands. In New England, winter nor'easters bring heavy rain or snow and fierce winds. The blizzard of 1888 dumped 45 inches of snow on Connecticut's shores, and a near-equal amount farther north on the coast. Summer brings vitriolic thunderstorms with hail and lightning. Perfect storms, like the famed October 1993 event, can arise when weather systems collide in the worst way.

Severe hurricanes occasionally drive north along the coast. The hurricane of September 21, 1938, goes down in the record books as the worst in the Northeast. It arrived shortly after noon. Six states were devastated by the high winds and huge storm surges. The worst losses were felt on Long Island and in Connecticut and Rhode Island. More than 600 people died. The storm surge in Providence, Rhode Island, was 13.5 feet.

Among the worst casualties were lightkeepers, their family members, and the light stations they tended. A telegram sent to the Lighthouse Service by its district superintendent in Southern New England the day after the storm reported:

> PALMER ISLAND LIGHT DWELLING DESTROYED . . . KEEPER'S
> WIFE DROWNED . . . PRUDENCE ISLAND DWELLING AND
> FOGBELL TOWER DESTROYED . . . KEEPER'S WIFE AND BOY
> REPORTED DEAD . . . .BEAVERTAIL LIGHTKEEPER'S CHILD
> DROWNED. . .

The damage and loss of life in the report seemed endless. One of the saddest tales came from Whale Rock Light at the entrance to the West Passage of the Narragansett Bay, where keeper Walter Eberle made the supreme sacrifice. He stayed with his light until high winds caused the cast-iron lighthouse to collapse on itself. Storm waves washed the shattered tower out to sea. Eberle's body was never found. His wife and children, living in Newport, survived.

One of the casualties of the great hurricane of 1938 was Whale Rock Lighthouse in Rhode Island. Lightkeeper Walter Eberle died when the tower collapsed. *Photograph by Jonathan De Wire*

# Goat Island Lighthouse
## NEWPORT

To guide ships into busy Newport Harbor, a lighthouse was established on the northern end of Goat Island in 1824. The location of the small stone tower proved unsuitable and caused several shipping mishaps. In 1842, a breakwater was built off the tip of the island, and a new 29-foot stone tower was erected. A few years later, the old abandoned lighthouse was moved to Prudence Island.

The second light at Goat Island began service with lamps and reflectors but was converted to a fourth-order Fresnel lens in 1857. A new keeper's dwelling was built in 1864. A decade later, a fogbell was added. Working in tandem with the lighthouse was a minor beacon on the southern end of the island. It was relocated to a skeleton tower in 1912.

In 1921, after a submarine collided with the keeper's dwelling, it was torn down. The lighthouse was electrified, and its care passed to workers at a torpedo station that had been established on the island. They continued to operate the light until 1963, at which time it was automated. In recent years, a large hotel complex was built on the breakwater. The lighthouse, now officially called Newport Harbor Lighthouse, has been licensed to the American Lighthouse Foundation. The grounds are open all year.

**FOR MORE INFORMATION**
American Lighthouse Foundation
P.O. Box 889
Wells, ME 04090
207.646.0515
www.lighthousefoundation.org
info@lighthousefoundation.org

**DIRECTIONS**
From RI 138 on the east side of Newport Bridge, take the exit for America's Cup Avenue and drive south to the Goat Island Connector. Drive over the small bridge and park in the visitor area of the wharf. The lighthouse is accessed through hotel property, and hotel staff can provide instructions.

Dwarfed by the Newport Bridge, the 35-foot Goat Island Lighthouse has shone a beacon for vessels entering Newport Harbor since 1842. A keeper's house once stood beside the tower, but a submarine from the naval base in Newport collided with it in 1921, and it had to be torn down. *Photograph by Shirin Pagels*

# Hog Island Shoal Lighthouse
## PORTSMOUTH

**DIRECTIONS**
From RI 114 on the north side of Portsmouth, take Miller Street to its end. The lighthouse is visible in the distance.

In 1866, a private steamship company anchored a small lightboat off Hog Island to mark the dangerous shoal extending off the island's southern tip. The aid was ineffective. In 1886, Eel Grass Lightship was moved to the site from Fishers Island Sound at the eastern end of Long Island Sound. It served until 1901, when a lighthouse was built on the shoal. The 60-foot iron caisson sentinel was painted white and exhibited a fifth-order Fresnel lens. Within a short time, the brilliance was increased with a fourth-order lens. Due to the cramped quarters and the isolation, families were not permitted to live at the lighthouse.

The lighthouse was automated in 1964. The Coast Guard made repairs and repainted the exterior in 1995. In 2004, under the National Historic Lighthouse Preservation Act, the lighthouse became available for nonprofit ownership. No applicants came forward, so the lighthouse was put up for auction in 2006. The lighthouse is not open to the public. It can be seen on public boat cruises that depart from Warren or from the Prudence Island Ferry. From shore, the lighthouse can be seen from Portsmouth and from Mount Hope Bridge.

The 1901 Hog Island Shoal Lighthouse was a lonely assignment. The tower's first keeper was dismissed for drunkenness. Few of his successors enjoyed the place, and even today it lacks appeal. In 2004, the Department of Interior offered the lighthouse for adoption under the National Historic Lighthouse Preservation Act. There were no takers, and the sentinel was put up for auction to the highest bidder. *Photograph by Jonathan De Wire*

# Ida Lewis Rock Lighthouse
## NEWPORT

Also called Lime Rock, this site is well-known as the home of celebrated lady light-keeper Ida Lewis, who served from 1879 to 1911. The light was established in 1854 about 600 feet from the city of Newport. It was a simple stone tower. The keeper lived ashore and rowed to the site to tend it. In 1856, a 13-foot brick tower was built, connected to a spacious granite dwelling. The sixth-order Fresnel lens was situated in an upstairs alcove facing the harbor and was accessed easily from the house.

In 1924, Congress voted to rename the site Ida Lewis Rock Lighthouse. Three years later, the light was automated and placed on top of a skeleton tower next to the old lighthouse. The defunct lighthouse was sold to the Ida Lewis Yacht Club for $7,200, and a wooden walkway was constructed connecting the lighthouse to the shore. The skeleton tower beacon remained in service until 1963. The sixth-order lens is now on display at the yacht club.

Ida Lewis Yacht Club is not open to the public except for occasional special tours. It can be seen from public harbor cruises in Warren and Newport and from several shore points.

**FOR MORE INFORMATION**
Ida Lewis Yacht Club
www.ilyc.org

**DIRECTIONS**
Travel east on RI 138, cross Newport Bridge, and go south on America's Cup Avenue (which becomes one-way Thames Street) into Newport. Wend through town on Thames Street until you see Ida Lewis Yacht Club in the harbor. There is parking available along the street.

Outshone by Ida Lewis, its famous rescuer-keeper, the Lime Rock Light was no more than a lens lantern hung in an alcove in Lewis's bedroom window. Even so, it gave succor to the many small boats in Newport Harbor. Ida Lewis gained fame as a lifesaver and appeared in many newspapers and magazines during the late nineteenth century. She died in 1911 while on duty at the lighthouse. *Photograph by Jonathan De Wire*

# Nayatt Point Lighthouse
## BARRINGTON

Established in 1828, the first lighthouse at this site was a brick tower 23 feet tall and attached to a brick keeper's house. It warned mariners away from a treacherous shoal at the mouth of the Providence River. The tower was poorly constructed and too small. In 1855, a storm damaged it beyond repair. A new brick tower was constructed in 1856, abutting the old keeper's dwelling. The 25-foot square tower exhibited a fourth-order lens. It continued in service until 1868, at which time the U.S. Lighthouse Board decided a light on nearby Conimicut Point would better serve shipping. Conimicut's lightkeepers lived at Nayatt Point, since there was no dwelling at the new lighthouse.

In 1883, a new tower was built at Conimicut Point, and the keepers moved to its quarters. The empty Nayatt Point Lighthouse was sold in 1883 and has remained in private hands ever since. Several additions have been made to the house. A lens from an old lightship now occupies the lantern but is not lit. The lighthouse is on private property and is not open to the public. It can be seen from public boat trips departing from Warren.

Built in 1828 and maintained in excellent condition as a private home, the house adjoining Nayatt Point Light is the oldest lightkeeper's house in Rhode Island. The tower was added in 1856. Though inactive for many years, a decorative light is shown from the lantern on occasion. *Photograph by Darlene Cook*

# Plum Beach Lighthouse
## JAMESTOWN

In 1896, construction began in the West Passage of the Narragansett Bay on a lighthouse to mark shallows off Plum Point. Problems with the submarine foundation halted construction a year later. A red beacon was placed at the site until building resumed in 1898. The caisson lighthouse was completed in 1899. It exhibited a temporary light for a few months, until the fourth-order Fresnel lens arrived. The lens was fueled by kerosene and mounted on a mercury float. A fogbell hung from one side of the uppermost tier of the lighthouse.

Ice cracked the caisson in 1918. The caisson was repaired, and additional riprap was piled around the tower. The fierce 1938 hurricane damaged the tower again and nearly killed its two keepers. In 1941, with the opening of the Jamestown Bridge, the lighthouse was no longer needed. It was decommissioned and its lens was removed. It slowly deteriorated.

In 1973, an attempt was made to paint the exterior, but the job was halted after a worker became ill from exposure to bird guano. Not until 2003 did work resume, after a nonprofit group was granted federal funds to refurbish the exterior and to stabilize the foundation. A beacon was returned to the lantern. Currently, the lighthouse is not open to visitors. It can be seen from boat tours departing from Warren or from points along the shore.

**FOR MORE INFORMATION**
Friends of Plum Beach
Lighthouse
P.O. Box 1041
North Kingston, RI 02852
www.plumbeachlighthouse.org

**DIRECTIONS**
The lighthouse is visible from Jamestown Bridge on RI 138. (No parking or stopping is permitted on the bridge.) It is best observed from shore by taking the North Main Street exit off RI 138, then going left on Frigate Street, left on Beacon Street, right on Pickering Street, left on Helm Street, and right on Spindrift.

An eyesore for many years, the defunct Plum Beach Lighthouse was the victim of a lawsuit filed in 1984 by a state worker who became ill from bird droppings while painting the tower. The suit languished in court for years, but the worker finally won in 1998. The exterior of the tower has since been restored to its original beauty.
*Photograph by Jonathan De Wire*

# Petticoat Keepers

*The light is my child . . .*
Ida Lewis, Lightkeeper
Lime Rock Light, Rhode Island

The majority of lightkeepers were men. But into this man's world a few women dared to tread. They did the same work as men and were inspected with equal rigor, yet they were paid less and were usually appointed only when no suitable man could be found. When uniforms were instituted during the 1870s, women continued to wear dresses. And in the nineteenth century, when many lights and fog signals were mechanized, many female lightkeepers held on to their jobs. Records indicate that the women performed well, despite ungainly skirts and educational disadvantages.

Young Abbie Burgess kept Maine's Matinicus Twin Lights operating through a terrible storm, and saved her hens from drowning. *Photograph from the National Archives*

A few lighthouse women are legendary, but most are remembered as simple, hardworking lightkeepers. They earned their positions almost exclusively through kinship. Massachusetts keeper Jane Martin assisted her father at the twin lights on Baker's Island and then went on to become head keeper at Marblehead Light. Ida Lewis of Lime Rock Light in Newport, Rhode Island, succeeded her father. Due to Captain Lewis's illness, he was never able to fully tend the station, and Ida did all the work. Her mother was appointed for a time after the captain's death, and Ida succeeded her mother in 1878.

Abbie Burgess, who as a young girl helped her father at the twin lighthouses at Matinicus Rock, Maine, went on to become assistant keeper at the station. She married a lightkeeper and ended her career as an assistant at Whitehead Lighthouse. Her grave in Spruce Head, Maine, has a small lighthouse on it. Her biography, and that of Ida Lewis, is popular in classrooms today and encourages young girls to aspire to nontraditional roles.

Ida Lewis of Rhode Island's Lime Rock Light gained fame for her prowess as a rescuer. *Photograph from the Newport Historical Society*

Sisters could earn lightkeeping jobs as well, but most lady lightkeepers were either assistants to their husbands or were "lighthouse widows"—women whose lightkeeper husbands died on the job. Official records reveal little about them. For example, the list of keepers for Dutch Island Light in Rhode Island neglects to mention the first name of Mrs. M. Fife, who became lightkeeper in February 1878 after the death of her husband, keeper George Fife. Similarly, Mrs. L. Crawford was listed as having replaced her husband that same year at Goat Island Light in Newport Harbor. Mrs. John Spear followed her deceased husband as keeper at Eagle Island Light, Maine, in 1848.

From 1846 until 1849, Hannah Brayley was a paid assistant to her husband at Ned Point Light in Massachusetts. Mary Strout worked beside her husband at Portland Head Light during the 1870s. One of the last civilian women to serve was Marcy Bachini Dunbar, who succeeded her husband in 1969 at Prudence Island Light and who remained on duty until automation in 1972. The only Coast Guard woman appointed to a New England lighthouse was Karen McLean. She tended the Kennebec River Light Station during the mid-1980s.

Though the government seemed to have no reservations about putting women in charge at lighthouses, not everyone was pleased about it. At Chatham Light during the 1840s, complaints were made about Angeline Nickerson, who took over after her husband's death. Some citizens believed a woman should not be given a job when a man wanted it. Letters were written on Mrs. Nickerson's behalf, and President Zachary Taylor refused to remove her.

The work of women at lighthouses extended well beyond the tower. Limited by the times and by inferior social status, they were also expected to cook, wash, sew, garden, houseclean, tend livestock, and raise children. To think that they also found time to serve as assistants and full-time lightkeepers is a credit to their gender. Multitasking, fastidiousness, and patience were hallmarks of a good lightkeeper. Women found it easy to live up to those requirements.

# Point Judith Lighthouse
## NARRAGANSETT

**DIRECTIONS**
From US 1 at Wakefield, take RI 108 south to Ocean Road. Turn right and follow the road to the parking area at the lighthouse.

This point extends eastward to mark shoals at the entrance to both Block Island Sound and Narragansett Bay. A daybeacon was placed on the point during the 1700s. The first lighthouse was built at the site in 1810; it was a simple octagonal wooden tower with a wooden dwelling. The beacon flashed by means of an eclipser, which helped mariners distinguish it from the fixed light at Beavertail. The lighthouse was destroyed by a storm in 1815.

A 35-foot stone tower was built the following year. The eclipser was installed in the new tower, along with a new Lewis light with ten lamps and reflectors. In 1857, a new 51-foot octagonal stone lighthouse was built. It was connected to a brick residence by a covered walkway. The tower exhibited a fourth-order Fresnel lens. The upper half of the tower was painted brown, and the lower half was painted white. A fog signal was added in 1867. In 1917, an oil house was built to store kerosene.

After automation in 1954, the keeper's house was torn down. The 1937 Coast Guard station next to the lighthouse became a rental in 1995. Major repairs were done to the lighthouse in 2000. The grounds are open to visitors, but the house is private and the tower is closed.

Foghorns jutted from the fog signal house at Point Judith Light in 1910. (**Above** *Photograph from the author's collection*) The brownstone tower still exhibits its original fourth-order fixed lens, installed in 1857 when the lighthouse was built. Electric horns have replaced the old trumpets, and today they give a single loud blast every fifteen seconds. (**Left** *Photograph by Jonathan De Wire*)

# Pomham Rocks Lighthouse
## EAST PROVIDENCE

The rocks, which jut into the sea lane on the eastern shore of Providence River, were named for a Narragansett chief killed in King Phillip's War in 1676. The cottage-style lighthouse was established in 1871. The lantern exhibited a sixth-order Fresnel lens.

In 1900, a foghorn was installed. Local citizens objected to the raucous horn, which was replaced by a siren, and then later by a bell. The lantern was upgraded with a fourth-order lens in 1939.

Modern conveniences came late to the station, including telephone service in 1940 and electricity during the 1950s. A cistern that collected rain runoff continues to supply water today. The beacon was abandoned in 1974, and its lens was moved to the Custom House Maritime Museum in Newburyport, Massachusetts. The station was sold to Exxon Mobil Corporation in 1980, and caretakers took up residence in the house. A nonprofit group has begun work on restoring the structure, with financial help from Exxon Mobil Corporation. The lighthouse is not presently open to the public.

**FOR MORE INFORMATION**
Friends of Pomham Rocks Lighthouse
P.O. Box 15121
Riverside, RI 02915
www.lighthousefoundation.org/pomham2.cfm
pomhamrockslighthouse@yahoo.com

**DIRECTIONS**
From I-195, take exit 4 to Riverside (RI 103). Drive five miles to Bullocks Point and park in the East Bay Bike Path lot. Walk north on the path a short distance to view the lighthouse, which is just offshore.

A Mansard roof and wooden light tower top the keeper's dwelling of Pomham Rocks Lighthouse, which faces the Providence River. The tower was relit in 2006 after thirty-two years of darkness. It currently is undergoing restoration with funding donated by Exxon Mobil Corporation, owners of the island. *Photograph by Shirin Pagels*

# Poplar Point Lighthouse
## WICKFORD

Established in 1831 at the entrance to Wickford Harbor, this lighthouse was originally an octagonal wooden tower incorporated into the roof of a stone dwelling. Its fixed white light was furnished by eight lamps and reflectors. A fifth-order Fresnel lens fueled by lard oil replaced the old Lewis light in 1855. Problems with cold air and snow getting into the tower forced further improvements during the 1870s, including the installation of a new lantern with better access from the house.

In 1882, the lighthouse was decommissioned, and a new pier-head light in the harbor took over its duties. The new light was officially named Wickford Harbor Light, but local residents referred to it as Old Gay Rock Light. It served until 1930, and then was torn down.

Poplar Point Light was sold at public auction and remains in private hands. According to the American Lighthouse Foundation, it is the oldest wooden lighthouse still in existence in the United States. It is not open to the public and can be seen only by private boat, though there is a view from a breakwater at Sauga Point in Wickford. From Rt.1 in Wickford, turn right on Camp Avenue. Turn right on Shore Acres Avenue and proceed to Sauga Point.

Modernized by private owners, the Poplar Point Lighthouse has become a special waterside retreat facing Wickford Harbor. The lantern has been dark since 1892, and many modifications have been made to the original building. *Photograph by Jeremy D'Entremont*

# Prudence Island Lighthouse
## PRUDENCE ISLAND

Originally built on Goat Island in Newport Harbor in 1823, this lighthouse was moved to Prudence Island in 1851. From its new location on Sandy Point, the lighthouse warned of underwater ledges in the channel between Prudence Island and Portsmouth. The octagonal tower was granite and rose 25 feet tall. A wooden keeper's dwelling was connected to the tower by an elevated walkway. In 1857, the old lamps and reflectors were replaced by a fifth-order Fresnel lens. Then in 1885, a fogbell was added to the station. The bell was mounted in a wood-framed tower that held the clockworks for the automatic bell striker.

**FOR MORE INFORMATION**
Prudence Conservancy
P.O. Box 115
Prudence Island, RI 02872
www.prudenceconservancy.org

**DIRECTIONS**
Take the Prudence Island Ferry from Bristol to Prudence Island and hike to the lighthouse.

During the 1938 hurricane, the lightkeeper's wife and son and three other people drowned when the house was swept away. The light was damaged, but not irreparably. Shortly after the storm it was updated with a fourth-order Fresnel lens and an electric light. The old birdcage-style lantern, typical of early 1800s lighthouse construction, was left in place.

The station was automated in 1972 with a modern optic, and it remains active. It is not open to the public but is being restored by the Prudence Conservancy, which leases it from the Coast Guard.

Prudence Island Lighthouse originally stood on Goat Island in Newport but was moved to its present site in 1851. The contractor who relocated the tower marked each stone with a number so the tower could be reassembled accurately. When the tower was reassembled, workers painted it white to conceal the numbers. The tower has a stone stairway and birdcage-style lantern. *Photograph by Jeremy D'Entremont*

# Rose Island Lighthouse
## NEWPORT

**FOR MORE INFORMATION**
Rose Island Lighthouse
Foundation
P.O. Box 1419
Newport, RI 02840
401.847.4242
www.roseislandlighthouse.org

Named for its shape, which resembles a flower bud and stem, Rose Island sits between Jamestown and Newport in the Eastern Passage of Narragansett Bay. Its lighthouse keepers went ashore in the station boat for supplies, to take children to school, and to visit the doctor. There was plenty of work to do at the station, especially for keepers who owned livestock. One keeper was so fastidious that he whitewashed the stones around the station. *Photograph by Shirin Pagels*

A guide for the East Passage of the Narragansett Bay, this sentinel was lighted in 1870 on the west side of 17-acre Rose Island. It replaced a small light that had been maintained by the Bristol Steamboat Company. The French Second Empire design combined a wooden tower and keeper's dwelling and was equipped with a sixth-order Fresnel lens. It was stabilized by a stone seawall. A fogbell was added in 1885. Conversion to kerosene necessitated construction of a brick oil house in 1912.

In 1969, the completion of Newport Bridge made the lighthouse obsolete. It was decommissioned in 1971. A local university leased it for a time but could not prevent vandalism. Ownership of the lighthouse was returned to the federal government, which offered it to the city of Newport. With the help of a local nonprofit group, the lighthouse was slowly restored and made into a small museum with overnight accommodations. The beacon was relit as a private aid in 1993.

The city of Newport still owns the lighthouse, whereas the island is owned by the Rose Island Lighthouse Foundation. All wildlife and historic structures on the island are protected. The lighthouse can be seen from Newport Bridge, from public cruises departing from Warren and from Newport, and from a summer ferry that runs between Jamestown and Newport.

The lighthouse is accessible only by boat. The public is welcome for short visits or for overnight stays. Permission to visit must be secured from the Rose Island Lighthouse Foundation, which also provides transportation.

# Sakonnet Lighthouse
## LITTLE COMPTON

**B**uilt on Little Cormorant Rock in 1884, an iron and brick caisson lighthouse marked the entrance to the Sakonnet River. The lantern's fourth-order Fresnel lens flashed from 70 feet above sea level. It was painted white to show clearly in fog and against the gray waters of the area. Storms battered the tower on numerous occasions. A 1924 storm sent water over the lantern and damaged the tower. The 1938 hurricane completely inundated the lighthouse and left a crack in the caisson. Additional damage by Hurricane Carol in 1954 brought an end to the light. It was decommissioned and closed.

Part of the lens was given to the Little Compton Historical Society. The remaining panels are now exhibited at the Maine Lighthouse Museum. In 1961, the lighthouse was sold at auction to a private owner, who kept it painted but who was not able to do expensive repairs. It was donated to a nonprofit group in 1985, and restoration work began. The beacon was relit in 1997 with a modern plastic optic. The lighthouse is not open to the public but can be seen from shore or from a private boat.

**FOR MORE INFORMATION**
Friends of Sakonnet Point Light
P.O. Box 154
Little Compton, RI 02837

**DIRECTIONS**
From Tiverton, drive south on RI 77 to the beach at Sakonnet Point. The lighthouse is visible offshore about a half mile to the west.

The landing area of Sakonnet Light is clearly visible in this circa-1920 image. Keepers considered the station one of the worst assignments in New England, and it had a constant turnover of crew members. Stress from bad weather and isolation often made tempers flare. During the 1930s, two keepers got into an argument, and one pulled a knife from a kitchen drawer. He forced his comrade outside on the lower deck and locked the door. The man nearly froze to death before a fishing vessel picked him up two days later. The two men were transferred and were never stationed together again. *Photograph from the Coast Guard Archives*

# Warwick Lighthouse
## WARWICK

**DIRECTIONS**

From US 1 in Apponaug, turn right on RI 117 and then turn right again on Warwick Neck Road. Park along the street at the terminus and view the lighthouse through the gate.

The first lighthouse on Warwick Neck was a 30-foot wooden tower incorporated onto a stone house. It was built in 1826 to assist vessels moving between the mainland and Patience Island. Until 1856, the beacon consisted of lamps and reflectors. Then a fourth-order Fresnel lens took over. A fogbell was added in 1882; it was followed by a fog siren in 1907 and an electric horn in 1932.

In 1889, a new keeper's house was built, and the old dwelling beneath the tower became a barn. By 1930, the lighthouse was on the verge of collapse, due to age and erosion. A new cast-iron electrified lighthouse was built in 1932.

The 1938 hurricane caused severe erosion around the tower and threatened to undermine it. The sentinel was moved 50 feet away from shore and placed on a concrete foundation. In 1985, it was automated. The lens was replaced by a modern optic with a green flash that remains in operation. A Coast Guard family resides in the house. The lighthouse is not open to the public but can be seen by boat or from the end of Warwick Neck Road.

The cast-iron Warwick Lighthouse was a survivor of the destructive equinoctial hurricane of 1938. Hundreds of homes and summer cottages were destroyed near the tower, and erosion left its foundation exposed. A year after the storm, the lighthouse was lifted onto a wooden platform and rolled to a safer location away from shore. It now sits on a concrete foundation.
*Photograph by Elinor De Wire*

# Watch Hill Lighthouse
## WESTERLY

A fire beacon was established on this hill during the 1740s as a warning to vessels traveling in Fishers Island Sound. The light was moved to a 35-foot wooden tower in 1808. Its whale-oil lamps were an improvement. In 1827, to avoid confusion with nearby Stonington Lighthouse, an eclipsing light was installed.

The 1938 hurricane caused considerable damage to the station. It was repaired and continued to be staffed by the Coast Guard until 1986. The lens was then removed and replaced by a modern optic. The station was leased to a non-profit group a few years later, and the keeper's quarters became a rental. An endowment provides funds for the upkeep of the property.

**FOR MORE INFORMATION**
Watch Hill Lighthouse Keepers Association
14 Lighthouse Road
Watch Hill, RI 02891

**HOURS OF OPERATION**
The museum is open from 1:00 P.M. to 3:00 P.M. on Tuesdays and Thursdays in July and August.

**DIRECTIONS**
From RI 1A in Avondale, turn south on Watch Hill Road. Turn right on Wauwinett Road, left on Bay Street, and left on Larkin Street. The lighthouse is off Lighthouse Road, but the parking lot is restricted to seniors and handicapped visitors. All others must park along an adjoining street and walk to Lighthouse Road and the lighthouse.

Named for the watch that was kept on the point during King George's War during the 1740s, Watch Hill got its first lighthouse in 1808. A square granite tower replaced the original in 1854 after erosion carried away part of the point. It exhibited a fourth-order fixed Fresnel lens.
*Photograph by Shirin Pagels*

Chapter 5

# The Lighthouses of Connecticut

Twilight descends on the light tower at Five Mile Point in New Haven. The lighthouse is one of many octagonal designs built between 1764 and 1850. The tower's eight granite faces and conical shape are designed to give the tower a low center of gravity and to cut the constant wind that scours the shore here. *Photograph by Elinor De Wire*

# Avery Point Lighthouse
## GROTON

The octagonal 55-foot concrete block tower stands on Avery Point overlooking New London Harbor and the entrance to the Thames River. In 1943, Avery Point was deeded by the state of Connecticut to the Coast Guard from the estate of industrialist Morton F. Plant, with the stipulation that a beacon light be erected on the point. Avery Point Lighthouse was lit the following year with a fixed white beacon to mark the Pine Island Channel. It was the last lighthouse established in Connecticut.

In 1960, the beacon was changed to flashing green. It served until 1967, when the state took ownership of the property. The tower deteriorated badly until 2000, at which time a nonprofit group formed to save it. A complete overhaul of the lighthouse took place, and in 2006 the beacon was relit.

**FOR MORE INFORMATION**
Avery Point Lighthouse Society
P.O. Box 1552
Groton, CT 06340
203.445.5417
www.averypointlight.com

**DIRECTIONS**
From I-95, take exit 87 and follow it to a right turn on Benham Road. Take a left on Eastern Point Road and drive to the entrance to the University of Connecticut campus. Park on the waterfront loop and walk to the lighthouse.

Avery Point Light is shown in 1945, during its active years. A brief career as a navigational aid and the fact that it never had resident lightkeepers probably accounts for lack of interest in the tower. In recent years, however, a group of preservationists from the nearby community raised money to refurbish the lighthouse and to relight it. *Photograph by Ron Foster*

# Bridgeport Breakwater Lighthouse
## BRIDGEPORT

**DIRECTIONS**
The lighthouse can be seen close up from the Bridgeport to Port Jefferson ferry.

Also called Tongue Point Lighthouse, this cast-iron tower was built in 1891 at the end of a breakwater to guide ships into Bridgeport Harbor. It displayed a sixth-order lens illuminated by a single kerosene lamp and also had a fogbell. Lightkeepers lived away from the site and had to row to the tower each day to tend it. Eventually, one keeper built a small shack on the breakwater for storage and shelter.

In 1919, after mariners complained the breakwater was a hazard to ships entering the harbor, the lighthouse was moved inland to its current site. The diminutive sentinel stands only 21 feet tall and rests on a 10-foot concrete base. It was automated in 1954 and modernized with an acrylic beacon in 1988. It is not open to the public but remains an active aid.

The steamer *Park City* was shown passing Bridgeport Harbor Light in this vintage postcard view from the early 1900s. Keepers reached the lighthouse via a five-hundred-foot stone breakwater. In 1913, lightkeeper Flora McNeil told a newspaper reporter: "I've been out during snowstorms when the plank was so slippery it was scarcely possible to keep your footing and all you could see in front of you was the falling snow. You could hear the roar of water under your feet and see the snow melt as it touched the waves, but you could hardly more than guess where to put your next step." McNeil moonlighted as a manicurist to supplement her meager lightkeeper's salary of $300 per year. *Photograph from the collection of Jeremy D'Entremont*

# Faulkner's Island Lighthouse
## GUILFORD

**FOR MORE INFORMATION**
Faulkner's Light Brigade
P.O. Box 199
Guilford, CT 06437
203.453.8400

Completed in 1802, this was the second lighthouse in the state. It was built on an island five miles off the coast to mark shallows in Long Island Sound. The octagonal brownstone tower stood 46 feet tall and was complemented by a keeper's dwelling. The lantern at first held a spider lamp and later a Lewis light, which was installed circa 1820. A fourth-order Fresnel lens took over in 1871, at which time a small exterior stairway was built from an upper window to the lantern because the lens was too large to allow access from inside.

The keeper's house was rebuilt in 1871, but it burned to the ground in 1976. Two years later, the station was automated, and vandalism became a problem. In 1988, the lens was replaced by a modern acrylic optic. Defacing of the tower continued, and erosion was a threat as well.

In 1991, a nonprofit group formed to rescue the lighthouse. Restoration was completed in 1999, and an anti-erosion project is currently underway. The lighthouse is open for tours on special occasions. It must be accessed by boat.

The 1802 Faulkner's Island Light endures, despite severe erosion on the island's eastern shore and loss of the keeper's house in a 1976 fire. Coast Guard personnel released several pet rabbits during the fire and were unable to catch them after the flames were doused. The rabbits survived, and their progeny riddled the island with burrows. *Photograph by Elinor De Wire*

# Fayerweather Island Lighthouse
## BRIDGEPORT

**FOR MORE INFORMATION**
Black Rock Community Council
30 Quinlan Avenue
Bridgeport, CT 06605

**DIRECTIONS**
Fayerweather Island is attached to the mainland by a breakwater. To reach the lighthouse, take exit 26 from I-95 and go east to Iranistan Avenue. Turn right on Iranistan Avenue and follow it until it ends at the water. Turn right on Soundview Drive, which becomes Barnum Drive. At the end of Barnum Drive is Seaside Park and a parking area. Walk the breakwater to the lighthouse.

Also called Black Rock Harbor Light, this lighthouse was established in 1808 on a 40-foot wooden tower. A spider lamp fueled by whale oil produced a feeble beacon visible only a few miles. The tower was toppled in an 1821 hurricane.

Two years later, the present rubble-stone lighthouse was completed. It housed a Lewis light with eight lamps and fourteen reflectors until 1854, at which time the beacon was upgraded to a fifth-order Fresnel lens. The tower was abandoned in 1932 in favor of a modern offshore beacon.

Vandalism took a toll on the old sentinel. Although the lighthouse was deeded to the city of Bridgeport in 1934, it received no care. The keeper's house burned down in 1977. Local residents mounted a restoration effort in 1983, and the Black Rock Community Council added further improvements in 1998. The grounds are open to the public.

Abisha Woodward, a carpenter from New London, Connecticut, built a number of lighthouses in southern New England, including the tower at Fayerweather Island. The octagonal design was sturdy and functional. The station's best-known keeper was Catherine Moore, who began assisting her father when she was twelve and who took over as the official keeper from 1871 to 1878. Moore never went to school but was an avid reader and a talented carver of duck decoys. She is credited with saving twenty-one lives while at the lighthouse. *Photograph by Shirin Pagels*

# Five Mile Point Lighthouse
## New Haven

The original light marking New Haven Harbor shone from a short wooden tower constructed for $2,500 in 1805. Mariners complained that it was a poor light, barely visible on the approach to the harbor. Nevertheless, it served more than forty years. When its walls began to collapse, it was replaced in 1847 by a stalwart stone tower 70 feet tall. A brick keeper's house built in 1835 stood nearby. Oil lamps and reflectors provided the light until 1855, when a fourth-order Fresnel lens was installed. The station also had a fogbell.

The stone tower served only thirty years before being upstaged by Southwest Ledge Light, a caisson structure built on a breakwater. The old lighthouse stood empty until about 1900, at which time it was leased to a local resident who gave tours for a small fee. In 1922, the lighthouse was deeded to the city of New Haven, which established the grounds as Lighthouse Point Park in 1949. The exterior of the tower was restored in 1986. It is not open for tours.

**FOR MORE INFORMATION**
Lighthouse Point Park
2 Lighthouse Point Road
New Haven, CT 06512
203.946.8019

**HOURS OF OPERATION**
Lighthouse Point Park is open year-round from 7:00 A.M. until sunset.

**DIRECTIONS**
Travel on I-95 through New Haven and take exit 50N or 51S to Townsend Avenue. Turn right on Lighthouse Road. Follow signs to Lighthouse Point Park and the lighthouse. There is a $10 fee to enter the park between Memorial Day and Labor Day.

Five Mile Point Lighthouse lost its job and its lens to a breakwater light in 1877, but it continued to serve in a variety of non-navigational capacities until it became the centerpiece of a city park during the 1920s.
*Photograph by Elinor De Wire*

# Great Captain Island Lighthouse
## GREENWICH

First lit in 1830, this lighthouse guided ships into the dangerous bottleneck at the western end of Long Island Sound and warned mariners away from jutting Greenwich Point. It was originally a 30-foot stone tower with a separate keeper's dwelling, constructed at a cost of $2,800. A Lewis light provided the beacon.

An 1838 inspection of lighthouses revealed the poorly constructed tower was deteriorating. But due to changes in the administration of the Lighthouse Service and the financial burden of the Civil War, the tower was not rebuilt until 1868. The new stone sentinel incorporated the tower into the roof of a keeper's house. Its fourth-order Fresnel lens burned whale oil and showed a fixed light. Also included at the station were a barn and a cistern to collect rainwater.

In 1890, a steam fog whistle was installed. It was changed to a foghorn in 1905, and a second keeper was added in 1916 to help handle the extra work required by the horn. In 1970, the lighthouse was automated and replaced by a light on a steel skeleton tower. The town of Greenwich took over the empty station in 1973 and installed a resident caretaker. The lighthouse is on private land and is not open to the public. It is not visible from the mainland.

One of five lighthouses in the region built in an integral design of granite house and cast-iron tower, Great Captain Island Light was named for Captain Daniel Patrick, who bought the island in 1640 from local Native Americans for the sum of "twentie-five coates." *Photograph by Shirin Pagels*

# Greens Ledge Lighthouse
## NORWALK

Built in 1902 at a cost of $60,000, this 52-foot cast-iron caisson-style lighthouse marked a perilous shoal in the shipping lane leading into Sheffield Harbor. The lantern was fitted with a fifth-order lens, but within months it was apparent that the light was inadequate, and it was thus upgraded to a fourth-order lens.

**DIRECTIONS**
To reach the viewing area, take CT 136 south from Hope Dock and turn left on Bluff Avenue, which eventually becomes Yarmouth Drive. Turn left onto South Beach Drive.

Winter ice buildup in the area and subsequent spring ice floes caused many problems for vessels passing the lighthouse. Several of the tower's lightkeepers were cited for heroic rescues. The men also endured the horrific September 21, 1938, hurricane, which caused the tower to develop a slight tilt.

The lighthouse was automated during the late 1960s. It is not open to the public but can be viewed from Norwalk's South Beach Road between Noroton Point and Pine Point.

A peaceful Norwalk sunset dapples the sky behind Greens Ledge Light in shades of orange and purple. The ledge has a sordid past. Legend says that long before the lighthouse was built, the dead body of a pirate named Green was chained to the rocks as a warning to all who passed to eschew the criminal life. *Photograph by Shirin Pagels*

# The Lightkeeper

*Up there among the clouds, my father and the other keepers have to watch, night after night, through storms as well as pleasant weather, through summer and winter, the year round, from sunset to sunrise; so that the poor sailors may be warned off from danger.*

Annie Bell Hobbs
*Nursery,* 1876

Few occupations are as venerated and romanticized as lightkeeping. Despite what history records, an image persists of the white-whiskered, leather-faced keeper of the light, scrambling about on sea legs and toting a spyglass. While others slept, the keeper stood watch. When others fled from danger, he faced storm winds and waves head-on—a fearless, compassionate, grandfatherly figure much like Shirley Temple's lovable Captain January.

Fiction aside, lightkeepers would probably have passed unnoticed in society had it not been for their venerable occupation. Most were middle-aged, hardworking family men with a strong sense of duty. They earned little money and suffered deprivation at some sites, but they were admired in their day and are still loved as selfless symbols of humanity. They kept their homes neat as a pin, in anticipation of the regular white-glove inspections by the government. They trimmed wicks in the lantern and tolled the fogbell on murky days. They kept the tower brightly painted and shipshape. During storms and other catastrophes, they displayed courage and fortitude few of us could match. Without question, it was an honor to have a lightkeeper in the family.

In the early years, the job was relatively simple: light up at dark, trim the wicks and wipe the windows a few times a night, replenish the fuel in the lamps, then extinguish at dawn and clean the lantern and beacon for the coming night. If fog rolled in, the keeper sounded the bell. After the advent of the U.S. Lighthouse Board, lightkeepers were selected more carefully, and the job became more rigorous. A keeper had to know how to read, write, and cipher; how to handle a boat; and what

Though poorly paid and expected to work when others slept or took refuge from a storm, the lightkeeper was a respected and sometimes romanticized figure. Most were married men whose wives and children were devoted helpmates. *Photograph from the author's collection*

*Photograph by Jonathan De Wire*

to do in case of a shipwreck or other disaster. Most were expected to have some mechanical ability as well.

Not surprisingly, some other abilities came with the territory. Most lightkeepers could forecast the weather; knew how to fish, hunt, and farm to augment their income and provisions; were good, creative cooks and penny-pinchers; and could do basic first aid. They were often well-read and self-educated, with encouragement from circulating libraries and correspondence courses provided by the government. A few preached Sunday sermons to their families and crew and served as teachers for their children. Light stations such as Great Duck Island in Maine, where more than thirty people lived during the early 1900s, were small insular communities. The schoolhouse doubled as a church and also as a recreation hall.

Until the 1890s, lightkeepers' jobs were politically controlled. The party in office appointed the keepers. When the administration changed, the lightkeepers shifted as well. War veterans were at an advantage. So were sailors, fishermen, and friends of politicians. Women were appointed if they had some connection to the service, such as a husband, brother, or father who had served as a keeper. Sometimes the work was a family calling, with the job handed down through generations.

New England had many memorable lightkeepers, both men and women. It had the first lightkeeper in the colonies—George Worthylake, keeper of Boston Light in 1716—and the last Coast Guard keepers in the nation, relieved from Boston Light in 1995. To single out just one in profile here would be an injustice. They collectively made our shores the safest and most welcome in the world. Some are more famous than others; some have more exciting stories to tell. But all deserve our thanks for their steadfast service.

# Lynde Point Lighthouse
## OLD SAYBROOK

**DIRECTIONS**
Head north on I-95, take exit 67 to Elm Street, and turn right. Cross US 1 to Main Street, and follow signs for Saybrook Point and the dock. Both Lynde Point Light and Saybrook Breakwater Light can be seen in the distance from the dock.

This station was first established in 1803 with a 35-foot wooden tower and a wood-frame dwelling. The beacon was originally produced by spider lamps but later was changed to a Lewis light consisting of seven lamps and reflectors with small lenses positioned in front of them. The beam rarely showed more than nine miles.

Considered inadequate, the station was rebuilt in 1839. A 65-foot octagonal stone tower was constructed. Ten lamps were installed in the new tower. In 1852, the lighting apparatus was upgraded to a fourth-order Fresnel lens. In 1858, a new keeper's residence was built. The wooden stairway, rebuilt in 1868, still spirals up to the lantern around a center post.

The station was downgraded in 1890 when a fifth-order lens replaced the larger one. Electric lines were laid to the station in 1955. The Coast Guard built new keeper's quarters in 1966 but automated the station twelve years later. The lighthouse is not open to the public but can be seen from Saybrook Dock.

The Connecticut River is New England's largest waterway. Lynde Point Lighthouse went into service at the river entrance in August 1803. The point is named for William Lynde, a farmer who sold the land for the station to the federal government for $225. Mists rising from a nearby marsh obscured the light, and dirt was hauled in to fill in the wetland. In later years, a seawall was built around the tower. Ironically, in recent years, efforts have been made to restore the marsh and to reforest the point.
*Photograph by Elinor De Wire*

# Morgan Point Lighthouse
## NOANK

The earliest light at this site was a 25-foot granite tower built in 1831. It operated a Lewis light. A keeper's dwelling was built nearby. In 1855, a sixth-order Fresnel lens was installed to give the beacon a range of 12 miles. The lighthouse served until 1868, when it became too dilapidated to continue service.

**DIRECTIONS**
From I-95, take exit 88 and turn south. At the junction with Route 1, turn left and drive about two miles to Route 215. Turn right. Watch for signs to Esker Point.

It was replaced by a 52-foot sentinel that incorporated a cast-iron tower onto a two-story keeper's house. The lens was moved into the new tower. In 1919, the lighthouse was deactivated and sold to private owners, but the lens remained in place. Some historians believe the optic was destroyed when horrific winds from the equinoctial hurricane of 1938 tore off the lantern.

The present owner had a new lantern fabricated using original blueprints. The lighthouse is not open to the public and sits in a private community. It can be seen in the distance from Esker Point Beach in Noank.

Lawn chairs face Fishers Island Sound at Morgan Point Lighthouse. The sentinel was sold to a private buyer in 1922. A local historian claims the lantern was destroyed during the 1938 hurricane, but other sources say it was removed prior to sale. A replica lantern was installed in 1991. *Photograph by Kraig Anderson*

# New London Harbor Lighthouse
## NEW LONDON

**FOR MORE INFORMATION**
New London Maritime Society
150 Bank Street
New London, CT 06320
860.447.2501

**DIRECTIONS**
Travel north on I-95 and take exit 82A, or travel south on I-95 and take exit 82B, to Colman Street and turn right. Turn left at Bank Street, then right at Shaw Street, and connect with Pequot Avenue. The lighthouse sits on the left near the end of Pequot Avenue. There is limited parking along the beach beyond the lighthouse.

This fourth lighthouse to be established in the colonies was built in 1761 at the entrance to the Thames River and the thriving whaling town of New London. The 64-foot stone tower replaced a simple beacon originally exhibited by local citizens. By 1800, the tower had cracked and was nearly in ruins. In 1801, it was rebuilt to a height of 89 feet, and a new keeper's residence and oil storage vault were added. The tapering octagonal tower exhibited eleven lamps and reflectors. In 1857, it was equipped with a fourth-order Fresnel lens. Six years later, the keeper's house was rebuilt. Both the house and tower remain standing today.

From about 1870 until 1911, the station was a testing site for fog signals. In 1911, its horn was moved to the New London Ledge Light in the Thames River estuary. The station was automated in 1912 with an acetylene gas light, and the dwelling was sold to private owners.

In 2005, the lighthouse was transferred to the New London Maritime Society under the terms of the National Historic Lighthouse Preservation Act of 2000. Although no public access has been established, several local charter companies operate occasional boat tours to area lighthouses.

*Connecticut's oldest and tallest lighthouse stands at New London Harbor. The station was quiet and removed from the bustle of town life during the 1880s when this photo was taken. Today it sits amid the sprawl of the city's suburbs and beams across the Thames River to a large industrial area and college campus. Photograph from the National Archives*

# New London Ledge Lighthouse
## NEW LONDON

In 1909, increased ferry traffic and the opening of a U.S. Navy base necessitated a beacon to mark the entrance to the Thames River. The Gothic Revival–style caisson lighthouse with a fourth-order Fresnel lens and fog siren cost $93,968. The structure sat a mile offshore, marking Southwest Ledge and rising 60 feet above sea level.

**FOR MORE INFORMATION**
Project Oceanology
1084 Shennecossett Road
Groton, CT 06340
860.445.9007
www.oceanology.org
oceanology@aol.com

The lighthouse was automated in 1987. Not only was it the last lighthouse built in Connecticut under the U.S. Lighthouse Service, but it was also the last lighthouse on Long Island Sound to be unmanned. After automation, the lighthouse was leased to the nonprofit New London Ledge Lighthouse Foundation for educational purposes. Public tours are offered periodically through Project Oceanology at Avery Point. The lighthouse can be seen from shore near New London Harbor Lighthouse and Avery Point Lighthouse.

Originally called Southwest Ledge Lighthouse, New London Ledge Lighthouse was renamed to avoid confusion with a New Haven sentinel of the same name. The one-of-a-kind design, costing nearly $94,000 to construct, was one of the most expensive lighthouses in New England. *Photograph by Elinor De Wire*

# Pecks Ledge Lighthouse
## NORWALK

A 54-foot cast-iron caisson-style lighthouse was built at the western end of Long Island Sound in 1906 to warn mariners of Pecks Ledge and shoals in the Norwalk Islands. It included a compressed air fog signal. The trilevel tower saw many changes in its lighting apparatus over the years. It first exhibited a fourth-order Fresnel lens illuminated with a kerosene lamp. The fuel was changed to incandescent oil vapor in 1932. A year later, the lens was removed in favor of a gas-powered aerobeacon, and the light was automated. In recent years, the light was solarized.

The lighthouse is not open to the public and is accessible only by private boat.

Caisson lighthouses, which stand in open water, were much like anchored ships. Nothing is more devastating on a ship than fire, and so it is with lighthouses. In 1913, lightkeeper Conrad Hawk left a vat of tar near his kitchen stove and went off in his boat to check another light in the harbor. He returned just in time to put out the flaming tar bucket. *Photograph by Shirin Pagels*

# Penfield Reef Lighthouse
## FAIRFIELD

Dangerous shoals off Penfield Beach known as the Cows and Calves spurred construction of this lighthouse in 1874. The design incorporated a wooden tower onto the roof of a granite dwelling that sat on a concrete pier. Due to swift currents in the area, 1,200 tons of riprap was laid around the submerged base of the pier to stabilize it.

**DIRECTIONS**
See directions for Fayerweather Island Lighthouse. Penfield Reef Lighthouse can be seen from Fayerweather Island.

A fourth-order lens was exhibited at the top of the 51-foot tower. It also had a fogbell mounted on one exterior wall. Due to the dangers of getting on and off the station, the lighthouse was a stag station, tended only by men whose families lived ashore. In December 1916, the principal keeper drowned while trying to row ashore to see his family for Christmas.

In 1969, the Coast Guard announced plans to raze the lighthouse and replace it with a modern monopole light. Government officials in the Connecticut congressional delegation fought to have the lighthouse saved. They were successful, and an automated modern beacon was installed in the tower in 1971. The lighthouse is not open to the public and is not accessible. It can be seen from Penfield Beach in Fairfield and from sightseeing cruises that depart from Captains Cove in Bridgeport. It can also be seen from Fayerweather Island.

In the 1868 *Annual Report* of the U.S. Lighthouse Board, a district lighthouse inspector called Penfield Reef "the most dangerous locality, during fogs and snow-storms, upon Long Island Sound." In 1874, the lighthouse was completed on a stone caisson stabilized with riprap. Solar panels now provide power for the light.
*Photograph by Shirin Pagels*

# Saybrook Breakwater Lighthouse
## OLD SAYBROOK

During the 1870s, two stone jetties were constructed at the entrance to the Connecticut River to define the shipping channel and to protect it from shifting sand. A 49-foot cast-iron lighthouse was built at the end of the west breakwater at a cost of $20,000. It began service in 1886 with a fifth-order Fresnel lens. A red panel was added to the lens in 1889 to warn of Crane Reef and a shoal called Hen and Chickens. A fogbell was also installed at this time. Only a year later, it was decided that a stronger light was needed, and the lens was upgraded to a fourth-order.

The lighthouse was damaged during the 1938 hurricane but was quickly repaired and placed back in service. Automation of the beacon occurred in 1959, but the Coast Guard continued to post a watch in the tower during bad weather. Extensive renovations were made in 1996 after this popular lighthouse was featured on a special state license plate. The lighthouse is not open to the public and can be seen only from private property or by boat.

The 1886 Saybrook Breakwater Light guides ships into the Connecticut River. *Photograph from the Coast Guard Archives*

# Sheffield Island Lighthouse
## NORWALK

To mark the entrance to the Norwalk River, a lighthouse was established in the Norwalk Islands in 1827. The 34-foot tower and stone keeper's dwelling were built on Sheffield Island. The fixed beacon consisted of ten oil lamps with reflectors. It was later changed to a revolving light. A red pane of glass in one lantern window varied the flash characteristic. In 1855, the sentinel was updated with a fourth-order Fresnel lens.

**FOR MORE INFORMATION**
Norwalk Seaport Association
132 Water Street
Norwalk, CT 06854
203.838.9444
www.seaport.org/Sheffield_island.htm
info@seaport.org

Even with a new lighting apparatus, the beacon remained ineffective. A new 46-foot lighthouse was built in 1868. The tower was incorporated onto a stone dwelling. By 1902, changes in the shipping channel rendered the lighthouse obsolete. It was extinguished, but personnel from Greens Ledge Light used the keeper's quarters.

The station was sold to a private owner in 1914. The Norwalk Seaport Association purchased the property in 1986 and restored it. Live-in caretakers began upkeep of the lighthouse and grounds. Annual public events supply critical funds to maintain the old lighthouse. Boat tours are available through the Norwalk Seaport Association, but times and dates vary. The lighthouse cannot be seen from shore.

Sheffield Island Lighthouse was a pleasant assignment for lightkeepers. The 53-acre island had plenty of space for gardening and livestock, and Norwalk was within easy reach by boat. But circa 1900, problems arose with the cistern, which sat too close to the privy. Germs leeched into the drinking water supply, and keeper Samuel Armour contracted typhoid. His wife looked after him and the station for many weeks until he recovered.
*Photograph by Shirin Pagels*

# Southwest Ledge Lighthouse
## NEW HAVEN

A handsome Second Empire–style caisson lighthouse was built in 1877 on a treacherous ledge at the entrance to New Haven Harbor. It consisted of a 45-foot iron house perched on top of a 12-foot iron and masonry foundation. Two cisterns for catching rainwater were housed inside the basement. A fourth-order revolving Fresnel lens provided the light, which was visible for 12 miles. A duplicate sister sentry of this lighthouse was built at the same time at Ship John Shoal in the Delaware Bay.

By 1888, the lighthouse had been painted red and had a foghorn. Stone breakwaters were built to enclose New Haven Harbor, and one of them extended out to the lighthouse. In 1889, one red pane of glass was installed in the lantern to warn of Branford Reef and Gangway Rock. The tower was automated in 1953. In 1988, its Fresnel lens was removed and replaced with a modern aerobeacon. It is not open to the public and can be seen only by boat.

Trees obscuring Five Mile Point Lighthouse in New Haven during the 1870s were a factor in the decision to build Southwest Ledge Lighthouse. It sits at the tip of a stone breakwater. An identical design was built at the same time on Ship John Shoal in the Delaware Bay. *Photograph by Shirin Pagels*

# Stamford Harbor Lighthouse
## STAMFORD

This picturesque white caisson lighthouse marking the channel into Stamford Harbor resembles a four-tier wedding cake. It was built in 1882 on Chatham Rock. Originally the tower was painted red, but by 1900 it wore a bright coat of white paint. The completed lighthouse stood seven stories high and exhibited a fourth-order Fresnel lens. It had a fogbell suspended from one side.

In 1949, the Coast Guard began attempts to close the lighthouse, believing it was no longer necessary for shipping. Each effort was thwarted by the public until 1953, when the lighthouse was automated for a short time with a green beacon and then officially decommissioned. It began to bounce back and forth between the General Services Administration and a series of private and municipal owners. Throughout this time, it continued to deteriorate. The lighthouse remains in private ownership and is not open to the public. It can be viewed by boat or can be seen distantly from shore in the Shippan Point area of Stamford.

A sketch of Stamford Harbor Lighthouse as it appeared in the late 1880s showed the boat landing and a chicken coop built by keeper Nahor Jones. Unfortunately a storm destroyed the landing and coop and drowned Jones's fowl. *Photograph from the author's collection*

# KEEPING THE KEEPERS

*They were the forgotten fleet of the federal government.*
Douglas Peterson, U.S. Coast Guard (Ret.)

With names like *Daisy, Lilac,* or *Azalea,* one hardly imagine a ship with a rough-cut crew that serves strenuous missions. Yet the lighthouse tenders were just such vessels—pretty names on homely hulks. The ships were the backbone of the U.S. Lighthouse Service. They built lighthouses, transported keepers and household goods, delivered provisions and mail, made repairs, and even brought the occasional medic, minister, or mother-in-law to a station.

Lighthouse Service vessels included a fleet of tenders that built, repaired, and provisioned lighthouses and lightships. Despite their rough-and-tumble crews, they wore pretty botanical names. *Cactus* was among the least attractive monikers. *Photograph from the Coast Guard Archives*

The botanical monikers were assigned during a ship's tenure as a vessel in the Navy's "Flowerpot Fleet." When the U.S. Lighthouse Board bought the ships from the Navy, they preserved the names. Small tenders had floral names, while the larger vessels were dubbed for shrubs and trees. The ships were fitted with cranes and winches and became the workhorses of the seaways. In addition to their duties at lighthouses, the ships tended buoys and fog signals, towed lightships on and off stations, and responded to emergencies.

The tender ensign was a triangular flag with a red border and a blue lighthouse on a white field. The ship's long, shrill whistle, sounded on the approach to a lighthouse, was the voice of both heaven and hell. It might bring a letter from a beloved family member or a long-awaited visitor, or it might bring the dreaded lighthouse inspector with his white gloves and critical eye. Children rushed to the dock with excitement when the whistle sounded. Mules and horses fled, knowing work was at hand hauling coal and other supplies.

Many a lightkeeper started his career as a tender crewman. It was hard physical work, and the ships rarely were in port. If a man longed to "swallow the anchor" and come ashore, a lighthouse was a good option. Since tender crewmen already were in the employ of the Lighthouse Service, they knew the nature of lighthouse duty and had an advantage over other applicants.

When the Coast Guard assumed control of lighthouses in 1939, it continued the tradition of the lighthouse tenders and their botanical names. The custom was recently broken with the launching of a Keeper Class of tenders that pay tribute to famous lighthouse keepers. Among the New England keepers honored are Ida Lewis, Abbie Burgess, Marcus Hanna, and Maria Bray.

Tender work today involves upkeep of the nation's many aids to navigation—lights, buoys, channel markers, Global Positioning System and vessel-monitoring towers, and other modern technologies for maritime guidance. One important aspect of the the tender's mission is gone: handling the needs of the lightkeepers and their families disappeared with automation.

# Stonington Harbor Lighthouse
## STONINGTON

Considerable shipping, whaling, and fishing activity near the small port of Stonington made a lighthouse necessary, and one was built in 1824. The 35-foot stone sentinel, with a lantern rising from a dwelling, was built for less than $3,000. The original lighthouse was dismantled in 1840 and was rebuilt some distance to the north. A hand-hewn granite spiral stairway in the new sentinel led to the lantern, where ten whale-oil lamps with reflectors provided the beacon. In 1856, these were replaced by a single lamp and a sixth-order Fresnel lens.

In 1889, the lighthouse was decommissioned and replaced with a 25-foot cast-iron light on a breakwater extending out from the harbor. This tower also had a fogbell. The keeper of the new light continued to use the old lighthouse as a dwelling. A new keeper's house was built in 1908. In 1926, the breakwater light was deactivated and razed.

By this time, the Stonington Historical Society had acquired the old lighthouse and began using it as a museum. Many of the displays were unrelated to lighthouse history, but gradually the old sentinel gained recognition. From its lantern, one can see New York and Rhode Island.

**FOR MORE INFORMATION**
Stonington Historical Society
P.O. Box 103
Stonington, CT 06378
860.535.1440
www.stonigntonhistory.org/light.htm
lighthouse@stoningtonhistory.org

**HOURS OF OPERATION**
The museum is open from 10:00 A.M. to 5:00 P.M. May through November and at other times by special arrangement.

**DIRECTIONS**
From I-95, take exit 91, turn south on Pequot Trail, and proceed to North Main Street. Turn left on North Main Street, cross Route 1, and continue to a stop sign and turn left. Turn right on Water Street. The lighthouse sits at the end of Water Street.

The 1840 Stonington Lighthouse contains blocks from its 1824 predecessor, which sat closer to shore. The lantern is accessed by a spiral granite stairway. From the top of the lighthouse, both Rhode Island and New York can be seen. *Photograph by Elinor De Wire*

# HOW TO BUILD A LIGHTHOUSE

*Here was the new lighthouse . . . in the shape of an egg . . . like the ovum of a sea monster floating upon the waves.*
Henry David Thoreau
Description of Minots Ledge Light, 1850

Lighthouses come in many shapes and sizes. The drawing board was versatile and sometimes clever. What determined lighthouse form and appearance? Location, function, budget, and era all contributed to the final decision. Science entered the formula, too— lighthouse engineers knew that a low center of gravity made for a more stable tower and that a conical shape cut the wind. An octagonal truncated cone shape proved one of the sturdiest designs, evidenced by the number of these towers still standing.

Location, function, and budget contributed to the appearance of a lighthouse. Bishop and Clerks Light in Massachusetts was a stalwart granite tower that sat on a rubble foundation on a dangerous ledge off southern Cape Cod. It had a bell tower alongside the light tower so that the weights that turned the bell's clockworks (similar to a cuckoo clock's weights) could drop. *Photograph from the Coast Guard Archives*

Most lighthouses built during the early years were wood. It was cheap and readily available, but it held up poorly in damp, salty air and was quickly dispatched by storm winds. Stone or brick became mainstay materials after 1800. There was an abundance of granite available in New England and many brick kilns. Air spaces in the walls of masonry towers were important to allow the lighthouses to breathe and stay dry. A birdcage-style lantern with many tiny windows was common, since early glass could be made only in small sheets. Better glass after 1850 meant bigger lantern windows. Stairways were wood or granite.

During the 1840s, northern foundries began cheaply producing iron, a durable and inexpensive material for construction. Iron lighthouses were manufactured in pieces, which were taken to sites for quick assembly. They could be moved easily if the shoreline changed. Most were given brick linings for stability. Lanterns and stairways also were iron.

Iron also was applied to the building of pile towers and screwpile towers, which consisted of a dwelling perched on heavily braced iron legs, either driven into a foundation or screwed down with flanged feet. They were suitable for alluvial soils and offshore sea-swept sites. The design allowed winds and waves to pass through the lower portion of the lighthouse unimpeded.

The caisson lighthouse moved offshore technology a step further with artificial foundations that supported light towers. These sentinels sat in the seaways, like traffic lights. Stone cribs came first, built directly onto the sea floor. Later, iron cylinders were fabricated ashore and towed to lighthouse sites, sunk, and filled with rock. These tough foundations could endure storms, ice, and even collisions by ships.

Reinforced concrete came into use by the time of World War I, but few sites in New England had concrete towers, since almost all lighthouses in the region were built before 1900. Fiberglass was used for a modern tower at Deer Island in 1982, but it was so unpopular with the public that the Coast Guard removed it.

Today, a plastic monopole with a solarized beacon and fog signal on top is the only requirement. Many lights of this style stand watch in New England, often unrecognized as a navigational aid except by mariners. They are lighthouses in a sense but stretch the definition. Most of us prefer a good, old-fashioned tower with a stairway spiraling to a lantern.

# Stratford Point Lighthouse
## STRATFORD

Marking a jutting point of land at the western entrance to the Housatonic River, this lighthouse first went into operation in 1821. It was an octagonal wooden tower that exhibited a cluster of oil lamps. Its eight walls were painted alternately back and white. Nearby stood a wooden keeper's house.

**DIRECTIONS**
From I-95, take exit 30. Follow CT 113 into Lordship and go left at Oak Bluff Avenue. Continue through a rotary onto Prospect Drive. The lighthouse is visible through a fenced area.

The beacon was upgraded numerous times, first with six Argand lamps in 1855, then with a fifth-order Fresnel lens in 1859, and finally with a third-order lens a few years later. A fogbell was added in 1864. The lens was changed once again in 1932 to a fourth-order. Alterations in the lens size reflected a rise and fall in shipping traffic over the years.

A new tower and keeper's dwelling were built in 1881. The 35-foot lighthouse was cast-iron lined with brick, and the dwelling was wood. In 1899, the tower was painted with a distinctive brown band around its middle. In 1969, the Fresnel lens was removed and replaced with a modern optic. The lantern also was removed. The lighthouse was automated in 1978, but the house continued to be used as quarters for the Coast Guard. In 1990, the lantern was returned to the tower for aesthetic purposes. The lighthouse is on private property but can be viewed from a distance.

Well-groomed Stratford Point Lighthouse wears a bold red sash to make it visible against a background of trees and white buildings. The station is home to a Coast Guard family.
*Photograph by Shirin Pagels*

# Stratford Shoal Lighthouse
## BRIDGEPORT

This comely Gothic Revival–style lighthouse sits on a stone pier marking dangerous Middleground Shoal in western Long Island Sound. It was preceded by a lightship that was anchored on the site from 1838 until the lighthouse was completed in 1877. The 35-foot stone tower originally showed a fourth-order Fresnel lens from 60 feet above sea level. It was considered a remote assignment and difficult to access. Keepers frequently were engaged in dramatic rescues, including a 1955 rescue that involved pulling a parachutist from the water.

The lighthouse was automated in 1970 with a modern optic. Repairs were made to the structure during the 1980s. It is not open to the public and can be seen only by boat.

A small beach, facetiously referred to by Coast Guard keepers as Waikiki, formed at the base of Stratford Shoal Lighthouse. The site was considered a difficult place to be stationed. In 1905, an assistant keeper went mad and attempted to kill his comrade and himself. *Photograph from the Coast Guard Archives*

# FLOATING LIGHTHOUSES

New England had a number of lightships between 1828 and 1985. The vessels worked much like light-houses, except they were anchored near danger points in the sea lanes, and their crews led double lives as sailors and lightkeepers. Day in and day out, they remained anchored in the same spot, showing a beacon and sounding a fog signal so that ships would avoid the area.

Many lightships were positioned around Cape Cod, marking its numerous shoals and shallows. The most famous was the Nantucket station, guarding what Congress in 1843 called "treacherous quicksands"—shoals stretching 35 miles southward from Nantucket Island. Notorious fog and winter storms in the area compounded the problem.

The first lightship in Nantucket was the *Nantucket South Shoal,* placed in operation about 200 miles east of New York City in 1854. She was a guidepost for almost all ships arriving from Europe via the North Atlantic sea lanes. Over the years, many lightships served at this spot. They rode out bad storms and endured the tedium of being anchored at the same spot for months at a time.

A lightship could serve in open water where a lighthouse might not be feasible. One of the most important lightship stations in New England was Nantucket Shoals, off the Massachusetts coast. The ship's name was painted on its hull, and its two masts, topped by light baskets, were easily visible for miles in all directions. *Photograph from the Coast Guard Archives*

The greatest danger for lightships was being rammed by another ship. At night or during periods of fog, other ships steered toward the sound of the lightship's fog signal, sometimes with disastrous results.

A vessel assigned to the shoals was only four years old when she went to the bottom following a collision. In January 1934, the ocean liner *Washington* sideswiped the *Nantucket #117.* There was little damage, but the crew was ruffled. Only four months later, in a dense fog, the huge passenger liner *Olympic,* sister ship of the *Titanic,* hit the lightship broadside. The *Olympic* was seventy-five times larger than the *Nantucket* and was traveling at about 20 knots. The *Nantucket* went down in only seven minutes, and four crewmen went with it. Another seven crewmen were rescued from the frigid water, but three of them later died.

The last vessel to serve on the shoals was the *Nantucket #612,* built at Curtis Bay, Maryland, in 1950 and in service at the station until 1983, when it was replaced by a large navigation buoy. It was decommissioned in 1985 and is now on display at Georges Island in Boston Harbor.

# Index

190

# About the Author

Elinor De Wire has been researching, photographing, and writing about lighthouses since 1972. She has visited more than 800 sentinels in the U.S., Canada, Mexico, the Caribbean, Europe, and Australia and is the author of thirteen books and more than 100 magazine and newspaper articles on the subject.

Elinor is the founder and charter president of the Washington Lightkeeper's Association and an advisory board member for several nonprofit lighthouse groups in her home state. She has been honored for her work in journalism, education, and historic preservation by the U.S. Lighthouse Society, the American Association of University Women, the American Lighthouse Foundation, New England Lighthouse Lovers, the Avery Point Lighthouse Society, the Florida Lighthouse Association, and the National League of American Pen Women. Three of her books have won Coast Guard Book Awards and the prestigious Ben Franklin Book Award.

Elinor resides in Seabeck, Washington, with her husband, Jonathan, a retired Navy officer, and her cat, *Lighthouse Kitty*, the mascot of "Kids on the Beam." Her two grown children, Jessica and Scott, have fond memories of the family's many travels to lighthouses.

## Acknowledgments

The author is grateful to the following people and organizations for assistance in the preparation of this book: Jeremy D'Entremont, Dr. Robert Browning, Chris Havern, Jeff Gales, Tim Harrison, Kathy Finnegan, Bob Trapani, Ron Foster, Sue Lott, Yvonne Zemotel, Kraig Anderson, Shirin Pagels, Bruce Robie, Sandy Clunies, Dave and Vicki Quinn, the National Archives, the Coast Guard Archives, and the men and women of the U.S. Coast Guard stations throughout New England who generously provided information and access to sites. Thanks also go to Kari Cornell for her skillful and cheerful editing guidance on this project, and to the crew at Voyageur Press for their professionalism and continuing interest in lighthouses. As always, I am grateful to my family—Jonathan, Jessica, Scott, Kristin, and Rebecca—for their support and encouragement.